DO NOT REMOVE
CARDS FROM POCKET

ALLEN COUNTY PUBLIC LIBRARY

FORT WAYNE, INDIANA 46802

You may return this book to any agency, branch,
or bookmobile of the Allen County Public Library.

ALL ABOUT
SEX THERAPY

ALL ABOUT SEX THERAPY

Peter R. Kilmann
Katherine H. Mills

PLENUM PRESS • NEW YORK AND LONDON

Library of Congress Cataloging in Publication Data

Kilmann, Peter R., 1945–
  All about sex therapy.

  Bibliography: p.
  Includes index.
  1. Sex therapy. 2. Sex therapy—Case studies. I. Mills, Katherine H., Date–   . II.
Title. [DNLM: 1. Sex disorders—Therapy—Popular works. WM 611 K48a]
RC556.K54 1983   616.85′8306   83-2257
ISBN 0-306-41317-5

First Printing—March 1983
Second Printing—September 1985

© 1983 Peter R. Kilmann and Katherine H. Mills
Plenum Press is a Division of
Plenum Publishing Corporation
233 Spring Street, New York, N.Y. 10013

Printed in the United States of America

PREFACE

This book was written primarily for members of the general public. It was not written with the professional in mind, although it is likely that some may learn new information about the scope and effectiveness of sex therapy. It is intended to provide an easily comprehensible overview of what sex therapy is, what it attempts to do, what it actually does, and the current issues in the field. The reader with a sex problem may learn some information which may help resolve it, but we must emphasize that this is *not* a self-help book or a substitute for sex therapy. The reader can, however, achieve a better understanding of sex problems, how they can be prevented, and what can be expected from sex therapy.

The average reader must realize that professionals differ among themselves in the definitions, causes, and in the ways to treat sex problems. In fact, among professionals, there are as many different ways to conduct sex therapy as there are clients. Thus, the reader should keep in mind that our descriptions of the way sex therapy is done represents what some sex therapists do, but we really do not know to what extent it is representative of all sex therapists.

Throughout this book, we illustrate our main points with examples of actual clients from our clinical files. Sex therapy is fairly straightforward in the treatment of some clients and very complicated in the treatment of others. Because some readers probably do not have a background in psychology, we purposefully simplified our description of the methods in some cases. We also attempted, as much as possible, to refrain from using technical language. When

5

this was a necessity, we explain the terms.

Many individuals have contributed in different ways to the development of this book. We would like to give a special acknowledgment to Dr. Bernie Zilbergeld who spent a great deal of time reading many drafts of the manuscript and offering very insightful feedback and structuring and shaping the final manuscript. His input had a very significant impact on the quality of this book. We also are grateful to Drs. Bernie Apfelbaum, Carol Rinkleib Ellison, Ernest Furchgott, Gary Haney, Lester Lefton, Howard Nankin, and Robert Sabalis for reading and offering helpful suggestions on drafts of the manuscript. Other readers who provided feedback on the book were Joe Boland, Chris Rogers, Sandy Sherman, Catherine Shortell, Melissa West and Kathy Zarek.

Among the various sources we used to write this book, we found Dr. Sandra Leiblum's presentation of the history of sex therapy, in Leiblum and Pervin's *Principles and Practice of Sex Therapy,* to be especially helpful in shaping Chapter 1. We also wish to express our thanks to Dr. Robert Chubon for his evaluation of Chapter 6. In addition, we found the personal vignettes in Bullard and Knight's *Sexuality and Physical Disability* valuable in enhancing Chapter 6.

We would like to give a special thanks to our secretary/typist, Oleta Beard, for her dedicated and enduring efforts throughout this project. We also are very grateful for the help of Edwa Meek, Heidi Edwards, and Patti Hunter-Kishline in typing and retyping many drafts of the manuscript. We would like to thank Bonnie Bella, Richard Milan, Gordon E. Brown, Laura Steckler, Ann Carol Price, and Richard Wanlass for their assistance in gathering the research.

We are most appreciative of the work of our editor, Linda Greenspan Regan, in coordinating this entire effort.

She provided much encouragement and guidance in completing the task.

We also are indebted to the many individuals we have seen in therapy who helped us gain insight into the diverse experiences of those with sexual problems. The names of the people in the case studies have been changed to ensure confidentiality, but we wish to thank those who have contributed to this book through sharing their personal experiences with us.

Finally, we would like to express our gratitude to friends and family who have provided emotional support and encouragement throughout this effort.

PRK
KHM

CONTENTS

ALL ABOUT
SEX THERAPY

Chapter One

SEX THERAPY
YESTERDAY AND TODAY

John and Diane had been married for five years before they had sex problems. John preferred a high frequency of sex. He would initiate two or three times each day even though Diane told him that having sex twice a week was just fine. Foreplay usually consisted of about three minutes of kissing and touching, after which John ejaculated. This was insufficient for Diane. Gradually she became less interested in sex even though she still participated to please her husband. However, she became openly critical of his inability to postpone his ejaculation more than 20 seconds after penetration. Eventually, John felt so angry at Diane for belittling him that he stopped initiating sex. Instead, he began to have an affair, rationalizing all the while that he needed to feel sexually desirable in order to feel important. Diane filed for divorce when she became aware of John's extramarital activities.

Fifteen years ago, many couples who had the same or similar sexual difficulties as John and Diane also would have ended their relationship or, at best, remained unhappy together. Today, however, an increasing number of individuals and couples with sexual problems are seeking treatment, commonly known as sex therapy.

The growth of sex therapy has corresponded with the increased media focus on sexual problems and what to do about them. Scan the issues of almost any newspaper or popular magazine, such as *Cosmopolitan, Ladies' Home Journal,* or *Newsweek;* inevitably, you will find an article or editorial about sexual problems. Self-help books and sexual

technique manuals have become best-sellers almost overnight. Popular sex magazines now discuss and give examples of a variety of sexual behaviors. These include bond-
age, discipline in the form of spanking, enemas, group sex,
and female and male homosexual experiences. Radio and
television talk shows often feature interviews and call-in
programs with sex therapists. From letters received by
newspaper and magazine columnists, it is apparent that
the American public has an insatiable thirst for further
knowledge about sexual problems and how to deal with
them. Professionals from many different fields—psychology, psychiatry, social work, nursing, and the ministry, to
name a few—often are deluged with requests for treatment
from individuals and couples with sexual complaints.

There are many reasons for the increased popularity
of sex therapy. Attitudes toward sex have changed dramat-
ically over the years, along with changes in other social
and cultural ideology. There is more emphasis placed on
sexual performance and sexual satisfaction today than was
experienced by our parents. Certainly, the treatment of
sexual problems has not always been so advertised or so
prevalent. How has sex therapy evolved?

Most of our historical accounts of the emergence of sex
therapy date back only as far as Victorian times. The sex
drive was considered dangerous, and it was believed to be
healthier to have little interest in sex. Sex therapy, such as
it was, focused on reducing sexual desire, stopping masturbation in children, and restricting sexual expression to
acceptable outlets, i.e., intercourse. As an extreme example
of such restrictive practices, in 1886, Richard von Krafft-
Ebing[1] reported applying a hot iron to a little girl's clitoris
to try to stop her from masturbating. He was unsuccessful
in curbing the girl's sexual practices but probably suc-
ceeded in producing both physical and psychological damage. Can you imagine how Krafft-Ebing and his contem-

poraries would have reacted to our common practice in sex therapy today of giving a client an assignment to masturbate?

Around the turn of the century, a few professionals attempted to present a more positive view of sex. Henry Havelock Ellis[2] viewed sexual desire as a natural human instinct that could be legitimately expressed in a variety of ways. He tried to move away from the idea that the desire for sex was dangerous and in need of strict control. Ellis recognized that women were sexual beings; he stressed the importance of foreplay, stimulation of the woman's clitoris, and prolonging intercourse to maximize a woman's sexual enjoyment.

Sigmund Freud, who was developing his psychoanalytic theory during this same time period, held very rigid guidelines for appropriate male and female roles in sex as well as in other areas of life. Freud was particularly restrictive of female sexuality. Sexual desire was considered to be a masculine phenomenon even if women happened to experience it. Women were thought to have "penis envy," and essentially were considered inferior to men, sexually and otherwise. As a female matured, she was supposed to shift her focus away from her clitoris to her vagina. Freud thought that a woman who continued to rely upon clitoral stimulation to become aroused and reach orgasm had underlying neurotic conflicts.[3] Although Freud usually completed therapy with his clients in a year or less, some of his psychoanalytic colleagues treated their patients for four or more years. A woman might have remained in analysis for five years without ever discussing directly her inability to reach orgasm.

Much criticism has been directed toward Freudian psychoanalysis for making clients conform to Freud's notions of "healthy" sexuality, which are considered rather narrow-minded today.[4] Yet much of sex therapy remained in this analytic mode until the advent of shorter-term directive therapies in the 1970s. It is only in the past decade or so that we have acknowledged that many "normal," otherwise well-adjusted adults experience sexual difficulties. Still, a number of therapists today continue to use a psychoanalytic approach in treating sexual problems. Some therapists, such as Helen Kaplan, have integrated a psychoanalytic approach and the more recently developed direct treatment methods of sex therapy.[5]

Some of Freud's female followers, such as Karen Horney and Mary Jane Sherfey, totally rejected his notions of female sexuality. They criticized his decidedly masculine bias and modified his personality theory to acknowledge that women are equal to men. A number of lesser-known, but still influential, women played an active role in freeing women from Victorian inhibitions.[6] Margaret Sanger was an ardent advocate of birth control which enabled women to have more control over their own bodies. Helena Wright, a gynecologist, was disturbed by the incredulous looks she received from female patients when she asked if they enjoyed sex. She felt that the widespread lack of sexual fulfillment in women was the result of guilt, shame, and anxiety related to sex, as well as ignorance of sexual techniques. She wrote several books,[7,8] first published in the 1930s, in which she explicitly instructed women on how to masturbate and how to reach orgasm during intercourse. The exercises she prescribed anticipated many of the methods used today to treat women with orgasm problems. For example, she suggested that once a woman learns how to masturbate herself, she may direct her husband's hand to show him how she likes to be touched.

In the 1920s and 1930s, the American public had an opportunity to receive knowledge about sexual techniques from the various "marriage manuals" that were published. The best-selling manual of that era was *Ideal Marriage*, first published in 1926 by Theodoor van de Velde.[9] It has been said that he "taught a whole generation how to copulate."[10] It is surprising to what degree van de Velde anticipated many of the sexual treatment methods that would become popular in the 1970s. Using experience derived from his medical practice, van de Velde emphasized acquiring a knowledge of sexual techniques in order to create a mutually satisfying marriage. He seemed more aware of the female sexual response than most of his male predecessors. He suggested prolonged foreplay until the woman was fully aroused, stimulating the clitoris both manually and orally, and whole-body caressing of both the man and the woman. He emphasized the mutual giving and receiving of sexual pleasure. Van de Velde also stressed the importance of variety to prevent sexual boredom in marriage. He gave detailed descriptions of different positions for intercourse and explained how a woman could exercise her vaginal muscles to increase pleasure for herself and her partner. Vaginal exercises are used today in the treatment of some female sexual problems. Perhaps the major point on which sex therapists would disagree with him was his ideal of the man and woman reaching simultaneous orgasms during intercourse. Today, this is considered an unrealistic and unnecessary goal that may only create anxiety and frustration for the couple.

In the 1930s, Robert Latou Dickinson, a gynecologist, emphasized that both spouses were responsible for making sex either satisfactory or unsatisfactory. He recognized the husband's role in contributing to female frigidity and incorporated this idea in his clinical practice. Dickinson also was one of the first to introduce the use of an electrical vibrator as a method of sexual stimulation for women. From surveys of his female patients, Dickinson and his associate, Lura Beam,[11] became aware of the sexual frustrations of many women. However, his work was not well publicized and therefore had little impact on the prevailing views of female sexuality.

In the mid-20th century, the publication of the Kinsey reports[12,13] had a great impact on the recognition of sexual behavior in America. From in-depth interviews with thousands of people across the country, Alfred Kinsey and his associates found that men and women masturbated, that most women readily reached orgasm from clitoral stimulation, and that women were indeed interested in sexual gratification. Among normal adults, it was not uncommon to find difficulties in sexual functioning.

The Kinsey reports made the American public realize that many more people were engaging in sexual behaviors than had been generally assumed. The findings, which were shocking to many people, established new standards for sexual behavior. Masturbation, oral sex, and sexual intercourse before marriage began to be recognized as "normal" in a statistical sense, even though these behaviors were still not considered acceptable or appropriate by many people. Kinsey's findings were highly publicized; in many ways, they gave the American public "permission" to lift the repression on sexuality. Formerly, the open discussion of sex had been considered taboo, even among scientific circles. Sex was a topic that was just not talked about! After the Kinsey reports, the public began to focus on sexual behavior as it never had before.

In the 1960s, the collective influence of the birth control pill, the feminist movement, and physiological research created an even greater focus on sexual behavior. The pill gave women, as well as men, the opportunity to enjoy sex without fear of an unexpected pregnancy. Partly as a consequence of the pill's availability, America began to witness a gradual liberalization of sexual behavior. More teenagers and young adults, especially women, began to engage in premarital sexual intercourse. Married couples began to have more frequent sex with more variation. Divorced men and women also had more frequent sex, and with more partners, than in prior years. The increased frequency of sexual behavior became associated with the term *sexual liberation movement*.

The feminist movement became more visible in the 1960s. As an outgrowth of feminists' influence, women became more aware of their capacity for sexual enjoyment and, indeed, their right to obtain sexual pleasure. A woman's inability to reach orgasm and a man's inability to delay ejaculation long enough to satisfy his partner became of greater concern to many individuals and couples. Many women began to resist the notion that sex was the exclusive province of men, or that a woman should submit to her husband's advances as a "duty."

The 1960s generally brought encouragement to move beyond restrictive cultural standards of sexual behavior. The "flower children" emphasized sensuality, pleasure-seeking, and "making love, not war." This provided further impetus for the American public to shed its Victorian shackles.

In 1966 the research of William Masters and Virginia Johnson offered new information about human sexual anatomy and physiology. Among their findings was the fact that on the average, the male becomes aroused to the point of ejaculation in much less time than the female becomes aroused to reach orgasm. This suggested the necessity for increased foreplay time to enhance the woman's likelihood of reaching orgasm. On a broader scale, their findings suggested that a problem in sexual functioning could be attributed to a couple's lack of awareness of the factors that influence sexual responsiveness. Masters and Johnson's research received widespread publicity, although more for their laboratory methods than for their results (i.e., they obtained their information by observing prostitutes and other paid volunteers engaging in sex, and they used cameras in artificial phalluses to assess physiological changes in women during the arousal process). Prior to 1970, the treatment of sex problems usually was considered a part of medical practice. Most sexual complaints were handled by gynecologists, urologists, or general practitioners. The more difficult cases typically were treated by a psychiatrist using psychoanalytic treatment. "Sex therapy" as an independent discipline did not yet exist. It was commonly believed that sex problems required many months and sometimes years of expensive and intensive therapy to "work through" numerous unconscious conflicts that interfered with the client's ability to function. The considerable time and financial commitment to treatment that psychoanalytic treatment required undoubtedly was a stumbling block for many people with sex problems. Although many therapists of the day claimed that clients who received long-term treatment resolved their sex problems, no substantial evidence in support of this claim was ever published. Several psychologists and physicians had tried some innovative, short-term methods to treat sex problems. Joseph Wolpe[15] and Arnold Lazarus[16] used the method of "systematic desensitization" to reduce the anxiety that interferes with a person's sexual response. James Semans[17] developed the "stop-start method," which teaches men with premature ejaculation to become more aware of and develop greater control over the sensations preceding ejaculation. Albert Ellis[18] emphasized the influence of an individual's beliefs on sexual functioning; he directed his therapy toward substituting rational for irrational beliefs about sexuality. However, these early short-term treatment approaches did not gain popularity. Lengthy psychoanalysis remained the dominant mode of treating sexual problems.

Then, in 1970, Masters and Johnson's *Human Sexual*

Inadequacy[19] was published. In this book, which is considered to mark the birth of short-term sex therapy, they defined in detail various male and female sexual problems. They suggested that the great majority of sex problems were attributed to psychological rather than physical factors. Yet they did not agree with the prevailing belief that individuals had sexual difficulties because of deep-seated psychological reasons. They also noted that in some cases, a combination of psychological and physical factors apparently contribute to sex problems, and, less frequently, that sex problems are totally due to physical factors. While many professionals now believe that Masters and Johnson underestimated the influence of physical factors on erection problems, especially for men in their later years, the notion that sex problems do not require long-term treatment represented an important departure from traditional thinking.

Perhaps what was considered Masters and Johnson's most meaningful contribution was their description of the innovative methods used to treat the sex problems of 790 males and females over an intensive two-week period. Very impressive results were offered as support for the effectiveness of these methods. As a consequence, Masters and Johnson were hailed as the founders of the new short-term sex therapy, a variety of methods apparently so powerful that amazing results could be achieved in only two weeks of intensive treatment and would be maintained five years after treatment ended! These results seemed utterly convincing to the many therapists who were looking for guidance in treating sex problems.

With all of the publicity given to the apparent effectiveness of short-term sex therapy, therapists from a variety of disciplines, such as psychiatry, psychology, and social work, began to pattern their treatment of sex problems after the Masters and Johnson program. Some attended workshops given throughout the country. Others traveled to St. Louis to be trained in these methods, which was quite an expensive venture. Many clients also spent a considerable amount of money in the belief that their sex problems could be treated successfully. Therapists, however, soon discovered that the sex problems of some clients resurfaced a short while after treatment ended. Even clients who seemed to need more sessions if they were to improve really didn't improve much, if at all, above the level of functioning that they had when they entered treatment; others even got worse. This was all very puzzling and frustrating at the same time. Why did many clients not maintain their gains over time? What was the problem? These methods were supposed to be extremely effective. Could highly positive results only be achieved by Masters and Johnson? What was wrong?

In 1980, Bernie Zilbergeld and Michael Evans[20] published an important article in *Psychology Today* that showed what was wrong. From a careful reading of *Human Sexual Inadequacy,* and from their own deductions, they discovered numerous problems in Masters and Johnson's reporting of their treatment methods and in the way their results were evaluated. Zilbergeld and Evans could not determine exactly what the therapists at the Masters and Johnson Institute actually did in their treatment, nor could they specify how many hours of treatment actually were conducted. Since specific criteria for successful treatment (we discuss this important issue in Chapter 7) were not mentioned, it could not be determined, for instance, whether a man who had an erection problem before treatment could gain an erection sufficient for penetration every time, every other time, once, or when, at the end of treatment. Their five-year follow-up included only 29% of the original number of clients. The fact that many couples either could not be contacted or refused to participate at the five-year follow-up indicated a lack of evidence that treatment really was as effective or long-lasting as had been presumed.

Why did the public and professional community accept Masters and Johnson's results without question for nearly 10 years? According to Zilbergeld and Evans, the solid reputation as pioneer sex researchers that Masters and Johnson had established from *Human Sexual Response* was somehow so pronounced that their subsequent work went unchallenged. It was evident that the American public was ready and willing for "brief sex therapy," especially since it was presented as being so effective by highly respected professionals such as Masters and Johnson.

Sex therapy has become popular largely because of its presumed effectiveness. It has offered hope for improving the sexual functioning of many individuals who, because of excessive anxiety about sexual performance and failure to obtain sexual satisfaction, began to consider sex to be a negative experience. Is the discipline really suspect because of the lack of confidence that can be placed in Masters and Johnson's results? Certainly, since 1970, many therapists other than Masters and Johnson have treated people with sex problems, and they continue to do so more and more. New methods of treating sexual problems have been developed. In the 1980s, therapists are treating the sex problems of many persons, including the elderly, homosexuals, and persons with various physical disabilities and medical conditions. How successful have these therapists been in making clients better? Can sex problems be treated effectively in a relatively short time? Which sex problems? What about the risks of receiving sex therapy? Can sex therapy be harmful? Thirteen years after the birth of sex therapy is sufficient time for us to evaluate the progress of the discipline.

It is our aim in this book to make a state-of-the-art report on sex therapy. We focus on the strengths and weaknesses of sex therapy, and on its complexity. We obtained our information from articles and books written by sex therapists, from our conversations with some of these people, from our own experiences in treating individuals and couples with sex problems, and from the research that has investigated sex therapy.

In the next chapter, we describe the methods of sex therapy while offering numerous examples of their use. Subsequently, we define and discuss the sex problems of various individuals. We mention some of the common factors that maintain sex problems, and we highlight some ways in which they are treated, using actual cases from our files. In Chapter 7, we present our conclusions of the effectiveness of sex therapy from our analyses of over 140 research studies. We offer some reasons why some individuals may benefit from receiving sex therapy while others may not. Finally, in the last chapter, we summarize the evolution of sex therapy and we discuss our concerns about the growth of the discipline.

REFERENCES

1. Richard von Krafft-Ebing, *Psychopathia Sexualis* (Stuttgart, 1886).
2. H. Havelock Ellis, *Studies in the Psychology of Sex* (New York: Modern Library, 1936).
3. S. Freud, *Three Essays on the Theory of Female Sexuality* (New York: Avon, 1962) (originally published, 1905).
4. S. R. Leiblum, L. A. Pervin, eds., *Principles and Practices of Sex Therapy* (New York: Guilford Press, 1980).
5. The most notable example of this integrated approach is H. S. Kaplan, *The New Sex Therapy* (New York: Brunner/Mazel, 1974).
6. More information about the contributions of these women can be found in E. M. Brecher, *The Sex Researchers* (Boston: Little, Brown, 1969).

7. Helena Wright, *The Sex Factor in Marriage*, 5th ed. (London: Ernest Benn, 1966).
8. Helena Wright, *More About the Sex Factor in Marriage*, 2nd ed. (London: Williams & Norgate, 1959).
9. Theodoor van de Velde, *Ideal Marriage, Its Physiology and Technique* (1926), trans. Stella Brown (New York: Random House, 1930).
10. E. M. Brecher, *The Sex Researchers* (Boston: Little, Brown, 1969).
11. Robert Latou Dickinson, Lura Beam, *The Single Woman: A Medical Study in Sex Education* (Baltimore: Williams and Wilkins, 1934).
12. A. C. Kinsey, W. B. Pomeroy, C. E. Martin, *Sexual Behavior in the Human Male* (Philadelphia: W. B. Saunders, 1948).
13. A. C. Kinsey, W. B. Pomeroy, C. E. Martin, P. H. Gebhard, *Sexual Behavior in the Human Female* (Philadelphia: W. B. Saunders, 1953).
14. W. H. Masters, V. E. Johnson, *Human Sexual Response* (Boston: Little, Brown, 1966).
15. J. Wolpe, *The Practice of Behavior Therapy* (Oxford: Pergamon, 1969).
16. A. A. Lazarus, "The Treatment of Chronic Frigidity by Systematic Desensitization," *Journal of Nervous and Mental Disease* 136 (1963), pp. 272–278.
17. J. Semans, "Premature Ejaculation: A New Approach," *Southern Medical Journal* 49 (1956), pp. 453–458.
18. Albert Ellis, "The Rationale Emotive Approach to Sex Therapy," *Counseling Psychologist* 5(1) (1975), pp. 14–21.
19. W. H. Masters, V. E. Johnson, *Human Sexual Inadequacy* (Boston: Little, Brown, 1970).
20. B. Zilbergeld, M. C. Evans, "The Inadequacy of Masters and Johnson," *Psychology Today* 14 (1980), pp. 29–43.

Chapter Two

THE METHODS OF SEX THERAPY

Sex therapy consists of a variety of methods. Some of these have been borrowed from other therapeutic models, such as behavior therapy and Gestalt therapy, and some have been developed specifically to treat sexual problems.

Which problems does sex therapy treat? After the publication of Masters and Johnson's *Human Sexual Inadequacy* in 1970, sex therapy most often treated problems in sexual functioning (sometimes called "sexual performance"). These were a man's failure to control when he ejaculates, a man's difficulty in gaining and maintaining an erection sufficient for penetration in intercourse, and a woman's failure to reach orgasm and to do it consistently. These sex problems still are the primary ones that sex therapy most often treats, with either the individual or the couple being treated. In recent years, however, sex therapy has evolved into also treating problems where there is no difficulty in actual functioning. These problems are a lack of desire for sex, a discrepancy in sexual desire between partners, a difficulty in becoming sexually aroused, an avoidance of sex, and/or an overall lack of sexual satisfaction. Much of sex therapy also involves a focus on helping individuals and couples to establish or reestablish a sexually and emotionally satisfying relationship. In the process of treating these concerns, sex therapy attempts to modify beliefs, attitudes, feelings, and behaviors that are presumed to be interfering with a person's sexual functioning and/or sexual satisfaction.

31

Sex therapy may be conducted in a mental health clinic, hospital, or medical center, in a university counseling center, or in the office of a private therapist. Typically, the client comes to the therapist's office once or twice a week for a therapy session, and any recommended sexual activity is carried out in the privacy of the client's own home.

The cost of sex therapy varies considerably. A few research projects have government funding and are able to provide treatment free of charge. However, most therapists charge a fee similar to that charged for the psychological treatment of other problems, such as depression. Many clinics and some private therapists use a sliding payment scale based upon income, ranging anywhere from five or ten dollars to one hundred dollars per hourly session. Clinics that specialize in sex therapy sometimes charge hundreds of dollars for weekend workshops, or thousands of dollars for intensive two-week programs; these fees far exceed the average cost of psychotherapy and seems to be the result of a high demand for such services. Unfortunately, it limits the availability of sex therapy to higher socioeconomic groups. Sex therapy typically is not covered by health insurance policies unless the therapist acknowledges that treatment has focused on other problems, such as a client's depression or anxiety.

WHO DOES SEX THERAPY?

Persons from a variety of professional backgrounds and training experiences treat people with sexual problems. Practically all are members of one or more of the following fields: the medical subspecialties of psychiatry and gynecology, clinical and counseling psychology, social work, marriage counseling, nursing, the ministry, and education. Some of these professionals treat only sex-related difficulties and hence label themselves as "sex therapists." Others also treat clients who have other problems, such as a person who is chronically anxious. These professionals may not necessarily label themselves as "sex therapists" *per se*, although they certainly may acknowledge that they treat sex problems. Throughout this book, we use the designation "sex therapist" to refer to a professional who treats sexual problems, regardless of whether the person also treats clients with problems unrelated to sexual functioning.

Considerable controversy prevails over who actually is qualified to treat individuals with sexual problems. Some of the controversy stems from the fact that sex therapy is not a unitary treatment but a variety of methods. Many professionals argue that sex therapy is a subspecialty of psychotherapy and therefore should be conducted only by a person who is recognized as a psychotherapist. This usually means a person with a graduate degree in psychology or social work, or a medical degree with a specialty in psychiatry. Yet some educators, sociologists, and clergy believe that they are qualified to treat sexual problems since treatment, by and large, involves educating individuals about various aspects of sexual functioning. Some of these persons believe that treating sexual problems does not necessarily require a graduate degree or a professional license.

One professional organization, the American Association of Sex Educators, Counselors, and Therapists (AASECT),[1] provides some standards for certifying professionals in the area of human sexuality. Certification as a "sex therapist" requires a master's degree plus three years of professional experience in the field or a doctorate with two years of experience. The therapist also must have completed 150 hours of sex therapy supervised by a professional. Standards for certification as a "sex counselor" or "sex educator" are less stringent. Over 1200 professionals in the United States are AASECT-certified as sex therapists. Another 400 have certification as sex counselors. About 1500 are AASECT-certified sex educators. It is likely that some of the professionals certified as sex counselors or sex educators provide sex therapy in one form or another, even though they may not refer to what they do as "sex therapy."

It is unclear how important AASECT certification really is. Because certification is voluntary, not all professionals who are competent in treating sexual dysfunctions are AASECT-certified. Some competent therapists who are not certified may be more effective than those who are, although this would be difficult to demonstrate.

There is no legal control over who can practice as a sex therapist. State licensure boards restrict unqualified individuals from using the title of psychologist or psychiatrist, yet anyone can claim to be a sex therapist or sex counselor. It is a safe assumption that most mental health professionals have not acquired the specialized skills necessary for conducting sex therapy. Workshops and lecture series are available to familiarize professionals with the factors that are thought to maintain sex problems, and how to use the specific methods of sex therapy. We believe, however, that adequate training for a sex therapist also should include direct and ongoing supervision of the therapist's clients by an experienced and qualified professional who is recognized as such by colleagues.

It makes sense for an individual or couple seeking treatment for a sexual problem to ask about the therapist's training, qualifications, and experience, rather than choosing any name from the phone book at random. Sometimes, finding the name of a qualified professional can be accomplished by contacting the department of psychology, psychiatry, or social work at a local university or medical school, or by asking a family physician, gynecologist, or urologist for a referral. It would be important to ask the referring physician whether many other patients have been similarly referred, and whether the physician has heard anything about the therapist's effectiveness. Friends or relatives who have received sex therapy and who had favorable reactions to their therapists also may help make this decision.

What happens when an individual or couple receives sex therapy? Typically, therapists begin treatment by conducting a sex history, although the scope of this method varies from one therapist to another.

THE SEX HISTORY

An accurate assessment of the problem is essential to planning the appropriate treatment strategy. Accordingly, in the sex history, the therapist attempts to identify the factors that may have caused and/or may be maintaining the problem. This includes a determination of whether physical factors are involved. The physical examination is very important in many cases, since some diseases and physical abnormalities can partially or totally be responsible for a sexual problem.[2] Therapists who are physicians typically perform a physical examination, while therapists who are not refer clients to a physician.

Drugs also can contribute to a sexual problem; over 100 drugs are thought to influence the sexual response.[3] Unfortunately, many pharmaceutical companies fail to mention the impact of their drugs on sexual functioning in their list of negative side effects. Nevertheless, some prescribed drugs do interfere with a man's ability to get an erection or a woman's ability to experience vaginal lubrication. Drugs seem to have highly individualized effects. Some persons who take low doses of drugs such as barbiturates, tranquilizers, and hallucinogens, become more relaxed and are able to function more successfully than at other times. Others who take these drugs have a high probability of experiencing a sexual problem. The client also is asked questions about alcohol intake. An excessive amount of alcohol can contribute to a sexual problem, such as a difficulty in gaining an erection, although alcohol seems to have individualized effects similar to drugs.

A few therapists also conduct a genital sensory examination, known as a "sexological," as part of the sex history. The examination, which is used for diagnostic and therapeutic purposes, helps each partner to discover the areas of the other's body that are most responsive to sexual stimulation. A sexological examination of a woman might contrast the sensitivity of the clitoris with the varying and usually less intense sensitivity of the different areas of her vagina. Most sex therapists, however, apparently don't do sexological examinations because controversy exists about whether therapist contact with a client's body is ethical. In fact, many sex therapists advocate a ban on the use of sexological examinations or any other methods that involve physical contact between the therapist and the client.[4]

The therapist obtains information on the possible psychological factors maintaining the sex problem. This includes a focus on the unique characteristics of the client or couple as individuals and as partners in a relationship. If the client is single, what is dating like? How has the client dealt with the sex problem? What is the client's adjustment to life in general? If a couple is being treated, what is the level of commitment of each partner to the relationship? How are conflicts dealt with? Are they resolved or are they left hanging in the air? Which conflicts may be contributing to the sex problem? What is the overall relationship like? How does each partner feel when in the presence of the other?

Clients also are asked for information about their sexual functioning. How often does sex occur? What actually happens in the typical sexual interaction? How long, on the average, are these activities engaged in? Is this acceptable? If not, why not? When does the client have a sexual problem? What is going on at the time? What is the client thinking and feeling? What are the partner's reactions to the sex problem? What are the client's goals for improved sexual functioning? How does the couple wish to change their sexual relationship?

Clients sometimes are asked to fill out forms to assist the therapist in getting information about the sexual history. On the following pages are some of these forms. It may be interesting to answer the questions as a way to gain an awareness of your own sexual history and sexual preferences.

Background Factors

Sometimes experiences in people's past affect the way they think and feel about sex. These questions are about your past experiences.

1. How affectionate were your parents?
    Toward each other
    Toward you

2. What messages did your parents give you about dating and sex when you were growing up?

3. What messages about sex did you get from other important influences during your upbringing?
   Peers
   Siblings
   Church
   School
   Other

4. When did you (Females: have your first menstrual period; Males: have your first "wet dream")?
   What were your feelings about this experience?

5. When did you first masturbate?
   What were you feeling about this experience?

6. When did you have your first sexual experience with another person?
   What was this like (behavior and feelings)?

7. Sexual experimentation with members of the same sex is quite common. Have you had any such experiences?
   If yes, what feelings did you have about this?
   When was your most recent such experience?

8. Have you ever had an unwanted pregnancy?
   If yes, how did you handle this?
   What were and are your feelings about this?

9. Have you ever been in a situation in which you were coerced to have sex?
   If yes, what happened?
   What were and are your feelings about this experience?

10. Are there any sexual experiences you have had that you feel guilty, uncomfortable, or angry about?

11. Can you think of any other past experiences that affect the way you think or feel about sex today?

Physical Factors

1. Are you currently taking any drugs or medication?
   Which ones (and for what)?

2. Have you been treated by a physician or surgeon for any medical problem during the past five years? Please describe.

3. Do you have any chronic or recurrent physical problems such as:
    Back pain
    Headaches
    Other pains (specify where)
    Fatigue, low energy
    Digestive problems (specify)
    Diabetes
    (For women) Gynecological problems (e.g., severe menstrual cramps, vaginal infections, cystitis, urethritis, prolapsed uterus, hysterectomy, menopausal symptoms)
    (For men) Problems with reproductive organs (e.g., prostate trouble, varicocelle, Peyronie's disease, urethritis)
    Other (specify)

4. How many days per week do you drink beer, wine, or hard liquor?

5. How much alcohol do you typically consume per week?

6. Are you taking any medications or recreational drugs? How often?

7. Can you think of any other physical or medical factors that might affect your sexual response?

Relationship Factors

1. How do you and your partner resolve sex-related conflicts that arise in your relationship (for example, one partner wants sex and the other is not in the mood)? Give examples.

2. Who do you see as the more giving partner in your sexual relationship?

3. Who do you see as the more affectionate partner?

4. Who do you see as enjoying sex more or being more interested in sex?

5. How well do you and your partner communicate about sexual issues? About nonsexual issues?

6. How would you characterize your feelings toward your partner (e.g., love him/her but not very sexually attracted, strong sexual feeling but not much emotional closeness)?

7. Are you currently involved in a sexual or romantic relationship with anyone other than your partner?
   If so, how serious is this relationship?
   Does your partner know about this?
   How committed are you to your partner?

Assessment of Level of Sexual Desire

1. How frequently *per month* do you *desire* (doesn't necessarily occur) to engage in sexual intercourse with your partner? _____

2. How frequently *per month* do you *desire* (doesn't necessarily occur) to engage in sexual activity (i.e., kissing, caressing, manual or oral–genital stimulation) other than sexual intercourse with your partner? _____

3. How frequently *per month* do you believe your partner desires (doesn't necessarily occur) to have sexual intercourse with you?
   _____

4. How frequently *per month* do you believe your partner desires (doesn't necessarily occur) to have sexual activity (i.e., kissing, caressing, manual or oral–genital stimulation) other than intercourse with you? _____

5. How frequently *per month* do you fantasize about sexual relations with your regular partner? _____

6. How frequently *per month* do you fantasize about sexual relations with someone other than your regular sex partner? _____

7. How frequently *per month* do you have erotic dreams that you can recall? _____

8. How frequently *per month* do you experience wet dreams?
   _____

9. (Males only) How frequently *per month* do you experience spontaneous erections without genital stimulation? _____

10. How frequently *per month* do you masturbate? _____

11. If you could choose any sex partner in the world, how many times *per month* would you desire to have sexual intercourse?
_____

12. Would you change (raise or lower) (specify which) your level of sexual desire or interest if you could? _____

13. Would you change (raise or lower) (specify which) your partner's level of sexual desire or interest if you could? _____

Characteristics of a Sexual Relationship

How characteristic of your sexual relationship are each of the following statements?

Very characteristic	Somewhat characteristic	A little characteristic	Not at all characteristic
3	2	1	0

Rating   *Comments*

_____ 1. Each of you can inform the other when you want to have sex.
_____

_____ 2. Each of you is interested in having sex. _____
_____

_____ 3. Each of you is able to relax during sex. _____
_____

_____ 4. You are not thinking about anything but what you and your partner are doing during sex. _____
_____

_____ 5. Each of you is able to become aroused during the sexual experience. _____
_____

_____ 6. You are able to understand your partner's cues about what
            is pleasurable sexually. _____

            _____

_____ 7. You and your partner decide which sexual activities are
            pleasurable. _____

            _____

_____ 8. You feel very positive about the sexual experience when it
            has ended. _____

            _____

Attitudes about Sex and Sex Roles

    Please indicate your own opinion of the statements below accord-
ing to this rating system:
    1. Strongly disagree
    2. Disagree somewhat
    3. Not sure
    4. Agree somewhat
    5. Strongly agree

_____ Masturbation is immature.
_____ Oral sex is enjoyable and perfectly acceptable to me.
_____ The use of fantasy during sexual relations is an enjoyable and
         harmless practice.
_____ The idea of having sexual relations during the menstrual flow
         is repulsive.
_____ The use of erotic literature or pictures to stimulate sexual arousal
         is perfectly acceptable to me.
_____ Initiation of sexual activity should be the primary responsibility
         of the male.
_____ Sexual positions in which the female is on top are unnatural.
_____ It is inappropriate or unacceptable for a woman to show very
         strong interest in sex.
_____ Women should satisfy the sexual needs of their partners and not
         be concerned about their own satisfaction.
_____ Premarital sex and extramarital sex are more acceptable for
         males than for females.

Sex Information Test

T   F   1. The sex drive in women declines steadily from about age 25 onward.
T   F   2. Masturbation can be damaging to one's health.
T   F   3. The clitoris is the most sensitive part of the female genitals.
T   F   4. Sexual problems are usually the result of serious psychological difficulties that can be traced back to childhood experiences.
T   F   5. Many men experience occasional difficulty in gaining or maintaining an erection.
T   F   6. There is no harm in having intercourse during the menstrual flow.
T   F   7. Most women are ready to have intercourse after 3–4 minutes of foreplay.

Actual and Preferred Settings for Sexual Relations

1. a. What time(s) of the day do you usually have sexual relations?

    _____

    b. What time(s) of the day would you prefer to have sexual relations? _____

    _____

2. a. What are the places in which you usually have sexual relations?

    _____

    b. What are the places in which you would prefer to have sexual relations? _____

    _____

3. a. What sounds (if any) are usually present during your sexual relations?
        Background sounds (e.g., music) _____
        Speech by you or your partner _____
        Nonverbal sounds made by you or your partner (e.g., moans) _____

    _____

b. What sounds (if any) would you prefer to have present during your sexual relations?
    Background sounds _____
    Speech by you or your partner _____
    Nonverbal sounds made by you or your partner_____
    _____

4. a. What smells or tastes (pleasant or unpleasant) are usually present during sexual relations (e.g., perfumes, body odors)? _____
    _____

    b. What smells or tastes would you prefer to be present during your sexual relations? _____
    _____

5. a. What type of lighting is usually present when you and your partner have sexual relations? _____
    _____

    b. What type of lighting would you prefer to be present when you and your partner have sexual relations? _____
    _____

6. a. What type of clothing are you and your partner typically wearing when sexual relations are initiated? _____
    _____

    b. What type of clothing would you like you and your partner to be wearing when sexual relations are initiated? _____
    _____

7. a. What type of erotic materials (e.g., pornography) or sexual aids (e.g., vibrators, K-Y jelly) do you and your partner typically use during your sexual relations? _____
    _____

    b. What type of erotic materials or sexual aids would you like to use during your sexual relations? _____
    _____

8.   What types of fantasies (if any) do you typically have during sexual relations? _____
    _____

Current Sexual Interaction

The following is a list of sexual behaviors. Using the first blank on the far left, please rank the behaviors in the sequence you typically follow in your current sexual interactions. Put a *1* beside the behavior you typically engage in first—e.g., *1* kissing male's neck; put a *2* beside the next behavior in sequence—e.g., *2* kissing (mouth), etc. Proceed until all of the behaviors you typically engage in are ranked. *Leave the behaviors you typically do not engage in blank.*

Sequence	Initiator	Time	Behavior
_____	M F	___	Kissing female's neck
_____	M F	___	Manual stimulation of male's breasts
_____	M F	___	Manual stimulation of female's genitals
_____	M F	___	Kissing/licking nongenital areas of female's body below the neck (e.g., back, stomach, legs)
_____	M F	___	Hugging
_____	M F	___	Kissing other parts of face on female (e.g., eyes, nose, cheeks)
_____	M F	___	Female masturbation (self-stimulation) during sex play
_____	M F	___	Oral–genital stimulation of male
_____	M F	___	Concurrent oral–genital stimulation of male and female (i.e., "69")
_____	M F	___	Male masturbation (self-stimulation) during sex play
_____	M F	___	Touching/rubbing abdomen on female
_____	M F	___	Kissing (mouth)
_____	M F	___	Touching/rubbing inner thigh of male
_____	M F	___	Kissing/licking nongenital areas on male's body below the neck (e.g., back, stomach, legs, toes)
_____	M F	___	Sexual intercourse—man on top
_____	M F	___	Oral–genital stimulation of female
_____	M F	___	Sexual intercourse—side entry
_____	M F	___	Rubbing fingers through female's hair (on head)
_____	M F	___	Manual stimulation of female's anus
_____	M F	___	French kissing
_____	M F	___	Touching/rubbing inner thigh of female
_____	M F	___	Oral stimulation of female's anus
_____	M F	___	Touching/rubbing abdomen on male

_____	M	F	—	Kissing or nibbling ear on female
_____	M	F	—	Sexual intercourse—rear entry
_____	M	F	—	Manual stimulation of male's genitals
_____	M	F	—	Manual stimulation of male's anus
_____	M	F	—	Anal intercourse
_____	M	F	—	Oral stimulation of female's breasts
_____	M	F	—	Kissing other parts of face on male (e.g., eyes, nose, cheeks)
_____	M	F	—	Sexual intercourse—female on top
_____	M	F	—	Oral stimulation of male's breasts
_____	M	F	—	Rubbing fingers through male's hair (on head)
_____	M	F	—	Oral stimulation of male's anus
_____	M	F	—	Manual stimulation of female's breasts
_____	M	F	—	Kissing male's neck
_____	M	F	—	Kissing or nibbling ear on male

Now, using the same list of sexual behaviors, please estimate the length of time you usually spend in each of the behaviors you just ranked. Record your estimate in the column labeled *Time*.

Next, using the same list of sexual behaviors, please indicate who typically initiates each of the behaviors. Circle the *M* that precedes the statement if the male usually initiates the behavior, or the *F* if the female typically initiates the behavior.

Ideal Sexual Interaction

Use the following list of sexual behaviors to describe your "ideal" sexual interaction. Put an *X* in the first blank on the left beside the sexual behaviors you would like to include in your ideal sexual interaction. You may indicate sexual behaviors you normally don't engage in but would like.

Check	*Time*	*Behavior*
—	—	Kissing female's neck
—	—	Manual stimulation of male's breasts
—	—	Manual stimulation of female's genitals
—	—	Kissing/licking nongenital areas on female's body below the neck (e.g., back, stomach, legs, toes)
—	—	Hugging

—	—	Kissing other parts of face on female (e.g., eyes, nose, cheeks)
—	—	Female masturbation (self-stimulation) during sex play
—	—	Oral–genital stimulation of male
—	—	Concurrent oral–genital stimulation of male and female (i.e., "69")
—	—	Male masturbation (self-stimulation) during sex play
—	—	Touching/rubbing abdomen on female
—	—	Kissing (mouth)
—	—	Touching/rubbing inner thigh of male
—	—	Kissing/licking nongenital areas on male's body below the neck (e.g., back, stomach, legs, toes)
—	—	Sexual intercourse—man on top
—	—	Oral–genital stimulation of female
—	—	Sexual intercourse—side entry
—	—	Rubbing fingers through female's hair (on head)
—	—	Manual stimulation of female's anus
—	—	French kissing
—	—	Touching/rubbing inner thigh of female
—	—	Oral stimulation of female's anus
—	—	Touching/rubbing abdomen on male
—	—	Kissing or nibbling ear on female
—	—	Sexual intercourse—rear entry
—	—	Manual stimulation of male's genitals
—	—	Manual stimulation of male's anus
—	—	Anal intercourse
—	—	Oral stimulation of female's breasts
—	—	Kissing other parts of face on male (e.g., eyes, nose, cheeks)
—	—	Sexual intercourse—female on top
—	—	Oral stimulation of male's breasts
—	—	Rubbing fingers through male's hair (on head)
—	—	Oral stimulation of male's anus
—	—	Manual stimulation of female's breasts
—	—	Kissing male's neck
—	—	Kissing or nibbling ear on male

Go back through the above list of behaviors again and indicate in the second blank the amount of time (in minutes) you ideally would like to spend engaging in that particular behavior.

TREATMENT METHODS

Many factors may contribute to sexual problems—anxiety, inadequate knowledge of sexual anatomy or sexual techniques, and difficulty resolving relationship conflicts, to name a few. It is for this reason that therapists have used a variety of treatment methods. Below we discuss the basic methods that, over the years, have characterized the essence of sex therapy: sex education, homework assignments, communication technique training, sexual technique training, and systematic desensitization. The reader should keep in mind that many therapists probably do not conduct the methods in such a structured fashion as they are presented. For many therapists, the methods are matched to the unique goals of the client.

Sex Education

Sex education may very well be the most important ingredient of sex therapy. Providing new information about various aspects of sex occurs throughout treatment. Audiovisual materials such as films, slide shows, and videotapes sometimes are used to explain aspects of sexual anatomy and physiology and to demonstrate sexual techniques.

In the first session, the man with premature ejaculation may learn much new information that directly relates to his difficulty. He may learn how common it is for men to experience occasional episodes of premature ejaculation. He may learn how he can practice delaying his ejaculation on his own. Depending upon his treatment goals, in subsequent sessions he may learn additional information, such as how to establish his personal conditions for feeling comfortable in a sexual interaction. If his premature ejaculation was maintained by a fear of not being able to perform adequately, he may learn various sexual techniques so that he feels more comfortable in providing sexual stimulation to a partner.

Sometimes, sex education involves informing clients of the necessity of modifying their treatment goals. Let us suppose that a woman enters her first therapy session with the goal of reaching orgasm every time she has intercourse. Many therapists likely would tell her that this goal might be too difficult to attain. She might be told that most women do not reach orgasm every time they have intercourse, and that many women do not reach orgasm through intercourse at all without concurrent clitoral hand stimulation. Her goals may then change into asking her partner for more foreplay time, and to stimulate her manually and orally.

Homework Assignments

An important method that seems to distinguish sex therapy from many of the other psychotherapies is the strong reliance on homework assignments. These are given so that clients can practice at home what they learn from the treatment sessions. Many therapists believe that homework assignments actually lessen the number of treatment sessions needed. Homework assignments may involve having the client read a book, or specific communication and sexual exercises.

Many therapists regularly give homework assignments to their clients, usually once per week. These assignments are given in gradual steps so that the client is able to learn or relearn to function sexually without the interference of anxiety or other psychological factors. The therapist only gives an assignment that is agreeable to the client and one that has a high likelihood of being completed successfully. This is because the therapist attempts to minimize the probability that the client will experience additional failure.

For some clients, the therapist may give a homework assignment with instructions *not* to engage in a particular behavior, especially if repeated failure has occurred. A man who has been unable to gain an erection sufficient for penetration in his last 10 attempts might be told to refrain from attempting intercourse, even if he thinks he will be able to penetrate. Sometimes, therapists attempt to gain the cooperation of the client's partner, either directly in the session or on the telephone, so that the partner does not sabotage the assignment by wanting the client to have intercourse too soon. This restriction may be lifted only when treatment has progressed to a point at which it would be logical for him to attempt intercourse. Other clients are encouraged to engage in any sexual activities that they would be comfortable with during the course of treatment. The decision about whether to ban a particular sexual activity during the early stages of treatment is an arbitrary one at the discretion of each therapist.

Therapists often ask clients about their thoughts and feelings while the homework assignments are being attempted. A man may be so concerned about his partner's evaluation of him while he is being touched that he cannot concentrate on the experience. A woman may begin to feel hostility toward her partner for being unfaithful to her in the past when she is asked to please him by stroking his body for 10 minutes. Therapy then might focus on these interfering factors before a direct focus on the sexual problem.

If the homework assignment is completed successfully, the therapist may give another assignment in accordance with the client's treatment goals. If any difficulties arose (such as the client's partner refusing to participate), this is discussed in detail. The therapist attempts to understand why the assignment was not completed. Was it too difficult? Would another one have been better? Which one? Perhaps some underlying conflict is blocking progress? If so, which conflict? This is where the skill of the therapist is so important.

The following excerpt from a session with a single female graduate student exemplifies some of these points. She had been sexually active for eight years but, due to reflexive contractions of her vaginal muscles (see section on vaginismus, Chapter 4), she had never been able to have intercourse. She did not have a sex partner. The therapist gave her homework assignments so that she would become familiar with her anatomy and would relax enough to reduce or eliminate the vaginal contractions. In the previous session, she had been instructed to insert one of her fingers into her vagina. She had not been able to complete this assignment in the past.

CLIENT: I was finally able to put my finger in all the way. I could even move it in and out!

THERAPIST: Good! You seem real pleased about it.

CLIENT: Yes. I'm really excited—maybe I can get over my problem after all!

THERAPIST: It feels like real progress?

CLIENT: Yeah, I thought about what we talked about with the right atmosphere and everything, and then it was so easy.

THERAPIST: Can you tell me more about that?

CLIENT: Well, I made sure that it was a time when my roommate wouldn't be around. Then I put on some soft jazz music and did the relaxation exercises you taught me. Then I started to touch myself and when I put my finger at my vaginal opening, I could just sort of slide it right in!

THERAPIST: What does that tell you about the circum-
             stances that are good for you sexually?
CLIENT: I guess that I need privacy. And candlelight
             and soft music help—I always fantasize about
             that with a guy when I masturbate. But the big-
             gest thing is being able to relax.
THERAPIST: You felt more relaxed when you tried the exer-
             cise this time?
CLIENT: Yeah. Those exercises really help me relax.
             And it was so neat—I never knew what was
             inside of me before! I felt this hard thing, like
             a bone, on the front side, and then deep inside
             there was this sort of fleshy hard thing. Are
             those normal?

The therapist then showed her a diagram of female
sexual anatomy, explaining the location and feeling of the
pubic bone, the cervix, and the vagina. Although she had
had a college-level sex education course in the past, the
structure of her sexual organs did not become real to her
until she explored it herself.

We have given the following homework assignments
to some couples who wanted to enhance their sexual relationship. These assignments were given only when they
seemed suitable for a couple's treatment goals.

1. Sit down with your partner and practice making verbal
   sexual initiations and refusals. Each of you should have
   at least three "turns" at both initiating and refusing or
   accepting. Provide feedback to each other on your reactions to the requests and refusals.
2. Set up a program or methods for dealing with conflicts in
   your relationship. Be sure to include the important principles of:
   a. choosing a proper time to discuss problems.
   b. sticking to one issue at a time.
   c. listening to your partner and thoughtfully consider-
      ing your requests and the motives underlying them.

  d. positively reinforcing your partner for having worked
      cooperatively with you in the effort to make your rela-
      tionship closer.
  Record your program and bring it with you to the next
  therapy session.
  3. Separately meditate about your sexual fantasies. When
     both of you are ready, share them. Then discuss whether
     or not your fantasy can be acted out or whether certain
     parts can be incorporated in your sexual relationship.

Communication Technique Training

     Many sexual problems can be attributed to difficulties
that one or both partners have in stating their sexual needs
in a direct, straightforward manner. For couples who have
problems with sexual initiations and refusals, the therapist
helps both members to communicate these more directly.
Each member is asked to verbalize to the other: "I would
like to have sex with you right now. How about it?" The
initiated partner then is instructed to respond either yes or
no. If the answer is no, the initiated partner is told that it
is important to give the reason why sex is being refused so
that the initiator does not misconstrue it. "Is my partner
mad at me?" "Does my partner have a headache?" "Is my
partner no longer interested in sex?"
     Next, each partner is asked to initiate as well as refuse
the other. One sequence that offers practice is for the initiated partner to first accept the other's initiation by saying
yes. The second time around, the initiated partner is
instructed to refuse the initiation by saying no. Finally, in
the third exchange, the initiated partner is instructed to say
either yes or no, and the initiator does not know in
advance which response will be given. After each partner
takes the role of the initiator and the role of the initiated,
the therapist suggests that these "initiation rules" should

be followed from then on. The therapist then might ask each partner's desired frequency for sex during the next week. If, for example, both partners desire sex more than twice, the therapist might encourage each to take responsibility for at least one of the initiations (assuming that this is acceptable to the couple). Other desired frequencies, such as those that involve specific sexual behaviors like oral sex, are negotiated accordingly.

Often, therapists also attempt to enhance the communication of nonsexual needs in a relationship. Many sex problems are at least partially attributed to partners being unable to resolve the disagreements that naturally occur from time to time. Typically, one or both partners have difficulty in asserting themselves. Somehow, requests go unheeded; either they are not understood or they are not acknowledged because of underlying hostility and resentment. This makes it extremely difficult for the couple to have a relaxed and pleasurable interaction. For these couples, the therapist may use George Bach's[5] fair-fight training methods to reduce the likelihood of unresolved issues interfering with sexual feelings.

Below is an example of a communication homework assignment. Each member of a couple is asked to make two lists. One list includes the specific behaviors that each partner likes in the sexual relationship. The second list includes the behaviors that each partner would like to change. Partners are asked not to show this list to each other until the next treatment session. At that time, the therapist insures that each item on the list is communicated in a direct, straightforward manner and that it is interpreted correctly by each partner. In this manner, partners learn new information about each other's reactions to the sexual relationship, and also practice giving such information to each other in a way that reduces the likelihood of confusion and misinterpretation. Below are the lists that were submitted by Ann and Jerry in response to such an assignment.

Ann's List of Positive Sexual Behaviors
> I like it when Jerry kisses me on my neck.
> I like it when he touches me softly and rubs me gently all over my body.
> I like it when sex is not planned, such as when I am woken up in the middle of the night or when he begins to touch me spontaneously.
> I like it when he kisses my breasts gently.
> I like it when he rubs my clitoris very easily.
> I like it when he spends a lot of time during foreplay.

Ann's List of Sexual Behaviors to Be Changed
> I would like you to kiss me more softly on my lips.
> I would like you to vary the speed of your thrusting in intercourse.
> I would like to have oral sex more often.
> I would like you to seduce me more often.

Jerry's List of Positive Sexual Behaviors
> I like it when you touch my penis softly.
> I like it when you sit on top of me during intercourse and rock back and forth.
> I like it when you kiss and touch my entire body.
> I like it when we try different intercourse positions.

Jerry's List of Sexual Behaviors to Be Changed
> I want you to spend more time kissing around my penis rather than just taking it in your mouth and sucking it.
> I would like you to kiss my chest more often.
> I would like it if you would kiss me during intercourse.
> I would like you to be more active during sex.

Sexual Technique Training

Specific sexual techniques often are suggested to help clients to reduce their focus on sexual performance, to dis-

cover more about their own and their partner's responsiveness to sexual stimulation, to gain a greater awareness
of their potential for sexual feelings, and to increase
mutual pleasure and satisfaction. At all times, the therapist
works within the client's or couple's framework for experimentation. Thus, sexual behaviors such as oral sex are not
likely to be assigned unless both partners are willing to
incorporate it in their repertoire.

A popular technique used to help clients become less
preoccupied with sexual performance is known as "sensate
focus."[6] A couple is instructed to find a time free from
stress and interruptions. They might be asked to undress
each other, with each partner alternating caressing, touching, and stroking the other's body. The therapist may suggest different ways to kiss and touch, or to manually stimulate the clitoris or penis. Couples initially are told to
refrain from touching the breasts or genitals. Intercourse
usually is prohibited until the couple is able to stroke and
touch one another in a mutually satisfying manner. In
essence, clients are encouraged to move away from a genital focus and to consider the entire body as a potential
playground for sexual pleasure.[7]

Below are several examples of sexual homework
assignments.

1. Develop a favorite sexual fantasy, including different
   aspects of having sex with your partner and focusing on
   nonintercourse activities such as touching and caressing.
   Find two times before the next session when you can feel
   relaxed and comfortable in thinking about your sexual
   fantasy and then begin to touch and stroke your genitals
   and your entire body. Try to discover what kind of stroking is most sexually arousing for you.
2. Take a relaxing bath or shower with your partner. Take
   turns washing and caressing each other's bodies, making
   sure that each person gets equal time and attention.

3. Place your hand over your partner's and direct him/her in the way that you like to have your genitals stroked and stimulated.

Systematic Desensitization

Systematic desensitization is a method that has been used for many years to treat individuals with anxiety reactions, such as a fear of heights, closed places, or crowds. Some sex therapists use the method to treat individuals whose anxiety in sexual situations interferes with their ability to function and/or obtain pleasure from sex.[8] The method uses relaxation to counteract the anxiety. The client constructs a hierarchy of sexual scenes, ranked in order of increasing anxiety, that reflects a desired sexual repertoire. The following hierarchy was used for a man with an erection problem.

1. You come home from work and your wife, dressed in an alluring black dress, greets you with an affectionate hug and kiss.
2. At dinner, your wife has prepared lasagna (your favorite meal) and serves it by candlelight with a bottle of wine and Frank Sinatra playing in the background. She appears in the mood to "make love."
3. After a long, intimate meal, you both enter the bedroom with thoughts of making love.
4. You begin kissing and hugging while you are both still fully clothed.
5. You and your wife slowly begin to undress each other.
6. You are both lying in bed naked, in each other's arms; you are both feeling "turned on."
7. It is early in foreplay; you are kissing and caressing one another; your partner is becoming excited.
8. Your wife begins to stroke your penis and appears very excited.

9. It is late in foreplay; your wife is showing that she wants to begin intercourse.
10. It is the moment of penetration.

The method begins with the therapist showing the client how to tense and relax various muscle groups throughout the body. Sexual scenes from the hierarchy list are presented to the relaxed client, starting with the scene that the client considers to be least anxiety-producing. The number of sessions required to complete the hierarchy varies, depending somewhat upon the client's ability to imagine the scenes and upon the intensity of the client's anxiety. Some therapists ask clients with a partner to attempt each scene with that partner as homework after it evokes only a minimal level of anxiety in the session.

Much of sex therapy is based upon the principles of systematic desensitization, even though some therapists do not use the term to describe what they do. Typically, the client is guided toward more positive sexual functioning in a step-by-step approach designed to minimize anxiety. The sensate focus exercises and other homework assignments described earlier in this chapter are examples of this approach.

THE CHOICE OF METHODS

How do therapists decide which of these methods to use, and when? We really don't know whether some of these methods are more effective than others for treating a particular sex problem. For instance, the treatment of a woman whose goal is to reach orgasm more consistently may include masturbation training instructions, systematic desensitization, one of these followed by the other, or some other method that involves enhancing sexual communication with a partner. Therapists usually just choose the methods they know how to use. The decision about when to use the methods seems to be an intuitive one for each therapist.

Sometimes, the client's goals for improvement influence the choice of methods. Some clients merely wish to obtain more sexual knowledge, such as, "I'm not sure how to turn on my partner. Can you give me some suggestions?" For these clients, sex education often is sufficient. Others wish to improve their ability to communicate with a partner about their preferences as to when and how they would like to have sex. The therapist, in these cases, may focus treatment exclusively on sexual communication. Other clients report an overwhelming degree of anxiety whenever they are confronted with a sexual opportunity; they wish they could relax enough to enjoy the experience. For these clients, the therapist may focus on reducing the client's anxiety in specific situations, perhaps using systematic desensitization.

In an increasing number of cases, sex therapists are finding that the successful treatment of the sexual problems of many clients requires a much broader focus than was thought necessary in 1970. For many clients, sex therapy no longer seems to be a simple matter of treating an orgasm or erection problem in a few sessions. Increasingly, therapists are discovering that treatment sometimes requires a focus on individual and/or relationship problems that contribute to the sexual problem. Some examples of these problems are presented below.

Individual versus Sexual Problems

Some clients are highly anxious in all situations, not just sexual ones. Others go through life in a depressed and melancholy mood. Some also lack confidence in social situations. They also may be excessively shy and feel inadequate in making contact with a potential partner. Some rarely, if ever, go on dates because of these concerns. For all of these persons, the therapist initially may forgo working on the sexual problem directly and instead may focus on how the individual's nonsexual problems may be interfering with the sex problem.

Other clients have a great deal of difficulty in letting themselves become emotionally close to a partner. They may have been badly hurt in one or more of their past relationships and they do not want to take a risk again. They are quite willing for a partner to trust them and take an emotional risk, but they are unwilling to reciprocate. Other clients go from bed to bed to bed looking for a sexual solution to their feelings of loneliness and alienation.

Sometimes, a client's feelings about relating to the opposite sex can block progress in overcoming a sexual problem. This is shown in an excerpt from a therapy session with a woman with vaginismus discussed earlier on page 35. She had been able to insert vaginal dilators of gradually increasing size during her homework sessions over several weeks (see Chapter 4). When she got to the dilator that was the size of a man's erect penis, she repeatedly had difficulty inserting it into her vagina. The therapist then explored her feelings about men.

CLIENT: I couldn't insert the dilator. It just wouldn't go in.

THERAPIST: What was the situation like when you tried it?

CLIENT: Well, I had a couple of hours between classes so I thought I'd try . . . but I was afraid that my roommate might be coming back any minute.

THERAPIST: Did you feel relaxed under those conditions?

CLIENT: No. I know that it wasn't a good time for me to do the exercise. But I just wanted to try any-

THERAPIST: way. I don't know if I'll ever be able to do it. I've tried so many times before.

THERAPIST: You sound discouraged [client nods]. What were you thinking and feeling when you tried to do the exercise this time?

CLIENT: Well ... I guess I was saying to myself, "This is never going to work, I can't do it." But then, I really wanted to and felt frustrated that I couldn't. I don't know ... maybe I'll never be able to have sex like everyone else.

THERAPIST: What would that mean to you?

CLIENT: I guess that I couldn't have a normal relationship with a guy. We could have sex and everything but when it came to intercourse, forget it! It's better just to stay away from those situations.

THERAPIST: So you're thinking that if you couldn't have intercourse, then it's best just to avoid relationships with guys?

CLIENT: Yeah, I may as well.

THERAPIST: Let's say that you were able to insert the largest dilator before you left town and we had to end therapy.

CLIENT: Well, then I would know that I could have intercourse.

THERAPIST: How might things be different then?

CLIENT: Well, I wouldn't have a good reason to stay away from guys. I guess that might have something to do with it. If I got my sexual problem straightened out completely, I guess I would still be scared to deal with guys. That rejection thing again.

The session then turned to a focus on her lack of trust in men, her fear of rejection, and her anxiety in dating situations. Eventually, she established a very positive relationship with a man and was able to have intercourse without difficulty.

Relationship versus Sexual Problems

Many couples who seek sex therapy are in distressed relationships. The presenting sexual complaint may involve a couple's concern about a man's erection problem or a woman's lack of ability to reach orgasm consistently from intercourse, but the therapist soon discovers that there is much beneath the surface. For instance, the man's erection problem may be a logical consequence of his wife's constant criticism of his unwillingness to spend more time with her. As the interview evolves, it becomes apparent that he avoids his wife because she is an extremely demanding person who does not let him know when he has done something to upset her except by means of a temper tantrum. He, in turn, always fuels her tantrum by doing exactly as he pleases without asking her for input on financial decisions. Similarly, a woman's orgasm problem may be attributed to the hostility that she feels toward her partner for his excessive attachment to his parents. This may have led to her long-standing belief that he considers his parents to be more of a priority than the relationship. She may think about this whenever they have sex, thus making it difficult, if not impossible, for her to become sufficiently aroused to reach orgasm.

In both of these cases, the therapist usually decides that an exclusive focus on the sex problem would be fruitless. Instead, efforts are made to discuss and move beyond these destructive interactions and established conflicts to determine whether each partner can make a commitment toward working on the sex problem. Once the air has been cleared, so to speak, the couple then can approach the sex problem with renewed energy. Of course, as we discuss in Chapter 7, not all relationship problems can be resolved.

For couples whose sex problem seems to be due to a lack of emotional closeness in the relationship, the therapist may give homework assignments focused on developing intimacy. The couple may be asked to have dinner together, to listen to music or take a walk together, and to freely ask each other what they are thinking and feeling at various times. The therapist may ask each partner to describe to the other when they feel fear, anger, joy, sadness, and love. In this manner, the couple begins to experience greater emotional closeness, which often corresponds with a greater desire for physical closeness.

In essence, it is now generally recognized that some clients require a broader treatment focus than was thought to be necessary 13 years ago. A woman who wants to reach orgasm more frequently may not show any improvement when the therapist focuses only on her orgasmic difficulty. She may improve only if treatment attempts to change her consistent pattern of choosing partners whom she does not really care about. A man who has difficulty in gaining an erection for intercourse may be able to show improvement only if he first resolves somewhat his fear of being controlled by women. Similarly, a woman who reports little interest in sex may begin to feel more comfortable having sex with her husband only after her hostility about having had intercourse against her will with her stepfather is dealt with in treatment.

Of course, the clients' goals for therapy are important in making the decision as to whether to treat the nonsexual or the sexual problems first. The individual or couple seeking treatment for a specific sexual problem sometimes is best served by initially getting what they want. Then, if this does not work (as is often shown by homework assignments not being completed or even attempted), the client might begin to see the importance of focusing on nonsexual problems before the sexual problem can be resolved. It has been our experience that nonsexual problems often need to be treated concurrently with, if not prior to, treating sexual problems.

HOW IS SEX THERAPY CONDUCTED?

The standard sex therapy format, as established by Masters and Johnson, consists of a male–female cotherapist team treating a couple. Many sex therapists have modified this format to accommodate the varied needs of clients requesting services. Sometimes, a client who does not have a sex partner is treated alone. In many cases, one therapist (rather than a cotherapist team) conducts treatment to save time and money and thus make services available to more people.

Some sex therapists treat groups of clients that typically include four to eight individuals or couples. The same treatment methods used for individuals or couples also are used in the group. Group members may not necessarily have the same sexual problem or the same goals. Discussions may center around communicating about sex or ways of enhancing sexual arousal. Group members usually share the progress they made or the difficulties they had in attempting their homework assignments. In some groups, the therapist holds brief sessions with each individual or couple to focus on unique problems and concerns.

The following is an excerpt from the second meeting of a group for women with orgasm problems and their husbands. This excerpt highlights how the members often support each other through the common sharing of experiences and feelings. It also shows how helpful it can be to include partners in treatment. In this session, the group leader had been presenting some of the possible factors that contribute to sexual problems.

MRS. A: After taking care of four kids all day, I'm usually just too tired for sex by bedtime. So when he touches me, I just cringe. I don't even want him to come near me.

THERAPIST: You think that if he touches you, that means he wants to have intercourse?

MRS. A: Yeah. And I'm just too tired for that.

THERAPIST: So you don't enjoy just kissing and touching him because you expect that will lead to intercourse?

MRS. A: Exactly! Every time he touches me, he wants to have sex.

MRS. B: I know exactly what you mean. It's gotten to the point now where I'm afraid to kiss my husband because then he'll want it. I can't even look at him lovingly without him wanting to go to bed. So I just avoid physical contact altogether. [All four women in the group are nodding their heads in agreement and the men are beginning to look uncomfortable.]

THERAPIST: It seems like this is a common experience amongst the group.

MRS. C: Yes, and even *after* we've had sex, I just want to touch and cuddle. But if I do touch him, he wants it again! [The women are all agreeing.]

THERAPIST: Any reactions from the men?

MR. A: Isn't it time to take a break?! [Everyone laughs.]

THERAPIST: Not yet. This discussion is making you a bit uncomfortable though.

MR. A: Yeah, but I don't know what to say. I guess

	it's true, but I didn't know that my wife felt that way.
Mr. C:	I know that I want sex a lot more often than my wife but I don't *always* want it. Sometimes she just rolls over in bed, and I don't know what's wrong. [Turning to his wife] I would be happy with just being close to you sometimes, even if you are not interested in having intercourse.
Mrs. C:	But it seems like that's always what you want when you touch me.
Mr. C:	Well, I guess it usually is! I figure I may as well try to see if you're interested.
Mr. D:	[Turning to his wife] See, it's not just me!
Therapist:	It seems like there are a couple of different issues involved in what you all are bringing up. One relates to viewing intercourse as the goal of every sexual encounter, the idea that sex equals intercourse. Men, especially, in our society have gotten the message to "get it when you can." [Everyone laughs and the men nod in agreement.]
Mr. D:	That's true. I don't usually think about sex without intercourse.
Mrs. D:	But sometimes I just want to be close to you without having intercourse. [The women nod in agreement.]
Therapist:	How do you let him know that?
Mrs. D:	Well, I guess I don't. I just withdraw from him.
Mr. C:	My wife does that too. [Turning to the therapist] Isn't communication an issue in this too?
Therapist:	Exactly! [The discussion then continues with a focus on sexual communication.]

Sexual Surrogates

The therapist may consider including a sexual surrogate in the treatment program when a client does not have a regular or cooperative sex partner, or when the client may be too shy to make contact with a partner. Some therapists in northern and southern California, and some in New York, use surrogate partners for some of their clients. Many more therapists throughout the country probably also use them, although this is not advertised due to potential negative publicity and possible ethical problems. The great majority of surrogates are women working with male clients. Male surrogates are rarely used for women but sometimes are used for homosexual clients. Most surrogates work with a few clients each week; they may be married or single.

If the client–surrogate relationship is considered mutually acceptable, the surrogate and the client might schedule weekly two-hour sessions away from the therapist's office. The therapist, client, and surrogate meet together after every client–surrogate session to discuss the progress of treatment. Any aspects of their interaction that may be anxiety-producing or problematic are discussed. The surrogate and the client attempt to closely approximate forming a relationship similar to one that might occur outside of therapy. For some clients, the surrogate's role in the early phases of treatment may involve teaching the client to initiate and maintain a conversation so that the client gains confidence and practice in making contact with others. Gradually they may have minimal physical contact such as kissing and touching. The surrogate does not always have intercourse with the client. This depends upon the client's goals. Sometimes the client has a successful intercourse experience with an outside partner, which makes it unnecessary to have intercourse with the surrogate.

Professionals are divided about the appropriateness of surrogate use. Advocates claim that a client without a cooperative partner is limited in the progress he or she can make in therapy. The relationship between the client and the surrogate is not considered to be primarily a sexual one but rather involves a prescribed series of interactions emphasizing communication and sensory awareness. With carefully trained surrogates, the client can learn social and sexual skills and develop the confidence needed to establish a satisfactory relationship outside of therapy.

Critics view the surrogate–client relationship as "unnatural" and, moreover, defeating the necessary step of having the client develop a personal relationship. How representative are the surrogate–client social interactions to relationships outside of treatment? What is the likelihood that successful sex with a surrogate will generalize to the client's ability to function successfully with outside partners? How can a surrogate–client relationship that is not stressful possibly approximate the stress associated with developing a real, potential relationship in a client's world? Critics also argue that surrogate use may violate the client's value system. They view surrogate therapy as a type of prostitution or sexual exploitation.

An additional drawback is that surrogate therapy is quite a bit more expensive than "regular sex therapy." The client must pay for the therapist's as well as the surrogate's time. If the surrogate and the client meet for two hours in the morning and if they both meet with the therapist later that day, the fee may be up to $200.

How necessary is the surrogate partner? For some clients, surrogates seem to be extremely helpful in offering an opportunity to practice specific social and sexual behaviors. By contrast, surrogate sex therapy may be contraindicated for clients who associate the expression of physical affection with deep emotional involvement.

What About Self-Help Books?

Numerous books are available to help individuals or couples either to solve their own sexual problems or to enhance their sexual relationships. Bernie Zilbergeld's *Male Sexuality*[9] and Lonnie Barbach's *For Yourself: The Fulfillment of Female Sexuality,*[10] and *For Each Other: Sharing Sexual Intimacy*[11] are popular examples. These books, which often are assigned by therapists as homework, include communication and sexual exercises. Many of our clients have found these books to be extremely informative and consider them to have been instrumental in facilitating their progress in therapy. Yet we do not know whether or to what extent individuals who have read these books without having received treatment from a therapist actually benefited. Some people, especially those who already are able to communicate about sex fairly easily with a partner and who do not have any incapacitating emotional problems, likely can improve their sexual functioning to some degree merely from reading a self-help book. For couples who have severe relationship problems, however, self-help books likely will not be sufficient to foster improved sexual fucntioning.

How Does Sex Therapy Differ from Other Psychotherapies?

Numerous similarities exist between sex therapy and some of the other psychotherapies. Yet sex therapy differs in some important ways.

Sex therapy is a very structured treatment, for the most part. The therapist typically employs a gradual, step-by-step approach to treat the sexual problem. A definite plan is followed, based upon the therapist's understanding of what is required. The therapist asks the questions, decides if the client's goals are realistic, plans the direction of treatment, and gives suggestions. In some of the other psychotherapies, the therapist is less active. Clients are given the freedom to bring up whatever issue they wish to discuss.

Sex therapy, for the most part, has a "here and now" focus in treatment. In some of the other psychotherapies, like psychoanalysis, the therapist may spend many sessions gathering extensive background information about the client's upbringing and specific past living experiences. An important part of treatment is to help the client, usually without much coaching, to understand the deep-seated or underlying presumed causes of the sexual problem. Thus, an orgasm problem would be treated by the therapist spending much time discussing the woman's relationships with her family members and even more time on her reactions to men in general.

In contrast, sex therapy works directly on the orgasm problem itself. The cause of the problem is not really very important if the therapist is able to understand, isolate, and treat what is maintaining it. Primarily, the sex therapist helps the client to substitute new sexual responses and behavior patterns for the ones that were thought to contribute to the problem. All of this is attempted without a lengthy treatment focus on the past. Certainly, the sex therapist is interested in obtaining information about the individual's or couple's background. However, this information usually is limited to obtaining the client's sexual history in a few hourly sessions at most. The therapist's questions usually are much more directed toward the present and the immediate past. How long have you been experiencing sexual difficulties? What was going on in your life when these difficulties began? What was it like for you the last time you had sex? Can you describe it to me? Who initiated sex? About how much time did you and your partner kiss and touch each other before you attempted penetration? What were you thinking about while this was going on? What were you thinking about when you penetrated? How were you feeling? About how long would you say that intercourse lasted? How did you feel afterwards? What do you think was your partner's reaction to the experience? These and other questions are asked to help the therapist understand more about the gap between current and desired sexual functioning or sexual satisfaction. Even when therapeutic issues in the client's past are uncovered, such as a woman's hostility toward her father, the relationship betwen those issues and the goal of experiencing a more positive sex life is always kept in mind.

Sex therapy is relatively short-term in comparison with the psychological treatment of problems such as depression; treatment usually is conducted for weekly one-hour sessions for two to six months. The number of treatment sessions that are needed usually depends, to a great extent, upon the problem and the client's goals, and the client's commitment to working on the problem (see Chapter 7). Sometimes clients need only one or a few sessions, especially if the goal is merely to learn accurate information about sex.

Sex therapy typically has as its goal specific behavioral changes in sexual functioning. Some of the other therapies have goals that are often vague and diffuse. These include helping a person to acknowledge feelings, to understand why conflicts may occur in social relationships, or to feel better about oneself. While all of these outcomes may, in

fact, correspond with positive changes in sexual functioning, these are not the primary goals of sex therapy.

Sex therapy uses specific changes in the client's sexual
behavior in accordance with the client's goals as guidelines
for the termination of treatment. Is the man who usually
ejaculated 10 seconds after penetration now able to last
three minutes or more? Is the woman who never had
reached orgasm now able to do so fairly consistently from
masturbation? Some of the other therapies do not offer the
client a specific index of when treatment can end. Psychoanalytic or dynamic therapists, for instance, often argue
that their treatments involve change on a much deeper
level than "superficial sex therapy." However, these therapists have not been able to demonstrate conclusively that
clients who receive "deep-level therapy" reach their treatment goals, nor have they been able to specify when, in
fact, this occurs.

Even though the methods of sex therapy appear to be
simple to some therapists who conduct other types of psychotherapy, a great deal of creativity and innovation is
necessary to treat each individual's or couple's unique sexual problems. No one method is equally applicable for all
clients. Should this particular couple first receive a focus
on sexual communication or specific sexual techniques?
Should the man with an erection problem be treated with
systematic desensitization alone or should the therapist
focus instead on the sexual and nonsexual communication
with his partner? What about the man who does not have
a partner? What should be done when a client does not
complete a homework assignment? Do you give the same
assignment again? Or do you give another one? The therapist's timing of when to say what is not a simple endeavor
either. How should the therapist confront the power struggle in this couple's relationship? What is the best way to
focus on this issue without alienating each partner or caus-

ing an overall disruption in the relationship? There are no hard and fast answers. In the following chapters, we show how these methods have been used to treat sexual problems.

REFERENCES

1. American Association of Sex Educators, Counselors, and Therapists, "Requirements for AASECT Certification," *AASECT Newsletter* 12(3) (1981), pp. 1–3.
2. A fairly comprehensive chart of various diseases and physical problems which influence sexual functioning can be found in H. S. Kaplan, *Disorders of Sexual Desire* (New York: Brunner/Mazel, 1979).
3. N. L. Story, "Sexual Dysfunction Resulting from Drug Side Effects," *Journal of Sex Research* 2 (1974), pp. 132–149.
4. J. LoPiccolo, "The Professionalization of Sex Therapy: Issues and Problems," in *Handbook of Sex Therapy*, ed. J. LoPiccolo and L. LoPiccolo (New York: Plenum, 1978).
5. G. Bach, Y. Bernhard, *Aggression Lab—The Fair-Fight Training Manual* (Dubuque, Iowa: Kendall/Hunt, 1971).
6. W. H. Masters, V. E. Johnson, *Human Sexual Inadequacy* (Boston: Little, Brown, 1970).
7. B. Roberts, "Surrogate Partners and Their Use in Sex Therapy," in *Sexuality in America: Contemporary Perspectives on Sexual Identity, Dysfunction and Treatment*, ed. D. E. Brown and C. Clary (Ann Arbor: Greenfield Books, 1981).
8. R. Auerbach, P. R. Kilmann, "The Effects of Group Desensitization on Secondary Erectile Failure," *Behavior Therapy* 8 (1977), pp. 330–339.
9. B. Zilbergeld, *Male Sexuality* (Boston: Little, Brown, 1978).
10. L. G. Barbach, *For Yourself: The Fulfillment of Female Sexuality* (Garden City, New York: Doubleday, 1975).
11. L. G. Barbach, *For Each Other: Sharing Sexual Intimacy* (Ann Arbor: Doubleday, 1981).

Chapter Three

MALE SEXUAL PROBLEMS

Most men (and women) in the American culture grow up with the expectation that sex is the man's domain. Men are expected to act confident when making sexual initiations and to know each and every way to please a partner. These and similar expectations place such a great deal of pressure on men that many have difficulty in sexual situations. In this chapter, we discuss premature ejaculation, erection problems, and ejaculatory inhibition.

PREMATURE EJACULATION

Jim was eagerly awaiting his forthcoming date with Cindy. He had dated her twice before but he had never made a sexual advance. But he thought that tonight would be the night. He had planned to take her to a popular nightclub for some dancing and drinks, and then back to his place. Promptly at 7:30 P.M., Jim picked Cindy up at her apartment. She wore a stunning dress and Jim immediately became aroused. At the nightclub, Cindy was very attentive to whatever Jim had to say. When they slow-danced, Cindy gave every indication that she would be interested in further contact. About midnight, Jim suggested that they watch a late-night movie at his apartment. Cindy agreed. Shortly after they arrived, Jim began to kiss Cindy and she seemed to enjoy this. As he began to touch and stroke her body, he realized that he was extremely aroused. They undressed each other and Jim felt even more turned on. But at the same time, he became anxious, wondering whether he would be able to last long enough to satisfy her. Once naked, both climbed into bed. Cindy began to stroke his penis. Realizing that he probably could not postpone his ejaculation much longer, Jim initiated intercourse. After two quick thrusts he ejaculated. Although Cindy didn't say a word, she gave a sigh of disappointment, which made Jim feel very inadequate.

Jim's experience is not atypical. Many men have a problem with premature ejaculation. Many women also complain that their partners don't last long enough. What is premature ejaculation anyway? When does a man ejaculate prematurely and when does he last long enough?

Premature ejaculation is somewhat difficult to define. Some therapists have defined it as a man's inability to delay his ejaculation after vaginal penetration long enough to "satisfy" a partner in at least 50% of his attempts.[1] A problem with this definition, however, is the meaning of the word *satisfied*. One woman may feel satisfied regardless of whether she reaches orgasm. Another woman may feel satisfied if she reaches orgasm manually or orally, but she may not necessarily be concerned if she does not reach orgasm during intercourse. Another woman may feel satisfied only if she reaches three or more orgasms during intercourse. Another problem with this definition is that many women probably would want to be "sexually satisfied" in more than 50% of their sexual interactions. And what about the man's satisfaction? A definition that depends upon the woman's satisfaction seems to be unfair to men. This is because some women reach orgasm during intercourse only if the experience lasts 20 minutes or longer. Still other women reach orgasm during intercourse very infrequently, if at all.

The question of exactly how long a man needs to last for a woman to feel satisfied (whether or not she reaches orgasm), and for the man to experience satisfaction as well, is difficult to answer in an absolute way. We do not believe that a time definition of premature ejaculation makes sense (i.e., a man's inability to delay ejaculation two minutes or longer during intercourse) for all men in all sexual interactions. Each couple's sexual interaction likely has different criteria for the man's sexual functioning in order for both partners to be satisfied. Thus, a premature ejaculation problem logically can be defined within the context of *each* couple's sexual interactions. If both partners are satisfied with the man's control over his ejaculation, whether or not the woman reaches orgasm, then the man would not be considered to have such a problem, at least in that relationship. In any case, a common denominator for men with premature ejaculation is that they are unable to delay their ejaculation when they want to.

What factors maintain premature ejaculation? Physical factors seem to be quite rare; they include prostatitis (an inflammation of the prostate gland), multiple sclerosis, and hardening of the arteries in elderly men. When a man consistently experiences premature ejaculation during masturbation, foreplay activities, and intercourse, the problem has a greater likelihood of being maintained by physical factors.

Premature ejaculation is almost always attributed to psychological factors, the most common one being anxiety. As in the case of Jim, mentioned above, during sex play the man may become anxious about his ability to really satisfy his partner. This often can distract him from recognizing the sensations leading to ejaculation. As a consequence, the man may lose control and ejaculate before he wants to. Some men attempt to postpone their ejaculation by focusing on anything except what they are doing, such as thinking about a baseball game, an iceberg, or a tragic event. Such efforts typically do not work; the man's attempt to avoid thinking about what he is doing often fosters so much anxiety that he loses control over his ejaculation anyway. Even if he can delay his ejaculation occasionally, he rarely enjoys the experience because of his preoccupation with lasting longer. And the unpredictable nature of when he can delay ejaculation and when he can't maintains his anxiety in any case.

Some men who are unable to delay their ejaculation generally don't have sex very often. When they do, they typically ejaculate fairly quickly since their penis is not accustomed to a partner's stimulation. However, some men who have sex quite frequently nevertheless have trouble delaying their ejaculation. Some of these men have a history of having sex under hurried, anxiety-producing circumstances. For instance, during adolescence and early adulthood, a man may have had sex only in the backseat of his car, in his parents' house, or some other place in which there was a good chance of being discovered; accordingly, he may always have tried to ejaculate as quickly as possible. Such a learned pattern of sexual responsiveness may persist even if the man eventually has sex in an anxiety-free setting, such as in his own apartment or in a motel room. Other men with premature ejaculation may have had partners who always gave them subtle cues to "hurry up and finish," thereby encouraging them to ejaculate quickly. It is uncertain why some men who have had sex under these circumstances eventually learn to delay their ejaculation while others continue to experience rapid ejaculation.

Some men with premature ejaculation have a history of unsuccessful relationships with women. Some are excessively shy and awkward in social situations. They have not had very many dates, or their dating history is very unsatisfactory. Some feel very uncomfortable about making sexual initiations or in their knowledge about sexual techniques. The uncertainty about what to do in a sexual situation leads some of these men to ejaculate rapidly.

The premature ejaculation of some men can be attributed to ongoing relationship problems. A man who is angry at his partner may not be interested in pleasing her. When the couple has sex, he ejaculates quickly because he is concerned only with his own gratification. In some cases, a woman who is not really interested in having sex may contribute to the problem by encouraging the man to ejaculate as soon as he penetrates rather than giving him a chance to feel in control of his responsiveness. During sex, she may stimulate him in the way that she knows will lead to rapid ejaculation. She does not really enjoy sex but she just wants to get it over with. Then, during an argument, the woman may remind him of his inability to last longer, and that she is never satisfied.

Treatment

Most men with a premature ejaculation problem recognize when they are losing voluntary control, but they seem unable to delay ejaculation. Two methods are most often used to help the man recognize the sensations that signify to him that he is getting close to ejaculation, and to help him delay his ejaculation: the *stop–start* or *pause* method and the *squeeze* method.

The stop–start or pause method was developed by James Semans in the 1950s.[2] The first step involves giving the man a homework assignment to choose a time and place when he can be in a relaxed frame of mind with no interruptions. He then focuses on a sexual fantasy that involves his partner (if he has a partner) or on some other arousing image while he strokes his penis in an up-and-down motion, simulating the stroking motion of intercourse. The man also might be told to change the amount of pressure that he is applying, change from an up-and-down stroking motion to circular motions, or slow down the pace of stimulation.[3] While he is doing this, he is instructed to focus on the sensations of arousal in his penis. He stops stroking just before he recognizes that he is getting close to the point of being unable to delay his ejaculation. He waits until he no longer has the urge to ejaculate. Then, he begins stimulating himself again. The man engages in this sequence three more times, and then he is told to continue on to ejaculation on the fourth time. The man is told to continue these exercises until he consistently is successful in delaying his ejaculation. It should be noted that the criterion for success likely differs from one therapist to another. We use the criterion of the man being able to complete the entire sequence successfully (i.e., ejaculating only after the fourth time) on three separate days consecutively within a one-week period.

Next, the man's partner (if he has one) is asked to assist in treatment. His partner is instructed to stroke his penis in the same way and in the same sequence as described above with his hand placed on her hand. The man is told to shut his eyes and imagine a sexually stimulating scene while his partner strokes him. Whenever he feels that he is close to losing control over his ejaculation, he is instructed to stop his partner's hand from stroking him. After he has regained control, she begins stroking him again. As in the exercise described above, this sequence is engaged in three more times, and then on the fourth time the man continues on to ejaculation.

Some men have more difficulty delaying their ejaculation when they touch a partner. These men might be told to touch a less arousing part of her body while the penis is being stroked. If this does not interfere with his ability to delay his ejaculation, the man then is told to touch a more arousing part of her body. For example, a man who tends to lose control over his ejaculation soon after he begins to touch his partner's breasts might be told to first stroke her arms and then her legs. If he still feels in control, he then proceeds to touching and then stroking her breasts. In this way, the man gradually experiences more and more stimulation while he practices delaying his ejaculation.

If these steps are completed successfully (we use the same criterion of success noted above), the next step involves teaching the man to delay his ejaculation during intercourse. Typically, the woman-on-top position is attempted first because it offers less direct stimulation for the man and thus is less likely to foster rapid ejaculation. This position also allows the man to control the woman's movements if he places his hands on her hips. (Of course, another intercourse position may be attempted first if the man reports a greater ability to delay his ejaculation in it.) The penis is inserted inside the vagina and the couple lies still until the man feels relaxed enough that he can delay his ejaculation. Then he moves his partner's hips up and down until he feels close to the point of ejaculation. At that time, he stops her hip-thrusting motions with his hands and lies still until he no longer has the urge to ejaculate. When he regains control, he begins to move his partner's hips until he again feels close to ejaculation. At this point, he stops her motions again. This procedure continues until he has been able to delay his ejaculation three times in a row, after which, on the fourth time, he attempts to ejaculate.

If this sequence is engaged in successfully (we use the same criterion as above), the next step involves the woman controlling the thrusting in the woman-on-top position with the man's hands on her hips. He is told to stop her thrusting whenever he feels that he is close to losing control over his ejaculation. The same sequence is followed as discussed above. If this is successful, the couple then is given the option of attempting other intercourse positions if they wish. Some therapists also recommend that the man test his newly developed control over his ejaculation by trying to ejaculate as quickly as possible during intercourse. This exercise, if completed successfully, demonstrates to the man that he has control over whether he ejaculates rapidly or whether he delays his ejaculation.

A modification of the stop–start method is the squeeze method developed by Masters and Johnson.[4] In this method, the man goes through the same exercises as with the stop–start method; however, when he feels the urge to ejaculate, he withdraws his penis from the vagina and he or his partner firmly squeezes the head of the penis. After the man feels in control again, the couple may continue to have intercourse.

Many people consider the squeeze method to be a disruptive inconvenience during intercourse. If the penis is not squeezed firmly enough, the man may ejaculate anyway; this outcome might discourage the couple from continuing to work on the problem. Some men feel very uncomfortable withdrawing the penis from the vagina and squeezing it, or asking a partner to do so. Some women are afraid to squeeze the penis because of the possibility of hurting the man. An advantage of the stop–start over the squeeze method is that it easily can be incorporated into the couple's sexual repertoire. Many couples enjoy having intercourse for a while, "taking a break," and then continuing on. For some couples, this pattern can lead to a relaxed and pleasurable sexual interaction.

Another method that sometimes has been used to delay ejaculation is to ask the man's partner to pull down on his scrotum and testes; this sometimes reduces the man's level of arousal and his urge to ejaculate.[5] However, this method may not be sufficient since it really doesn't give the man practice in delaying his ejaculation. Other methods for delaying ejaculation—thinking of anything but sex, the use of anesthetizing lotions and sprays—have been used but it is not clear whether or not these are effective. As far as we know, nothing works as well as the stop–start and squeeze methods for helping a man to delay his ejaculation.

In some cases, teaching the man to delay his ejaculation using the methods noted above is all that is necessary for resolving the sex problem. In many other cases, however, these methods are insufficient due to the presence of one or more individual or relationship problems. For a man who feels insecure and anxious in social and sexual situations with women, the therapist and the man may rehearse social conversations to make him feel more comfortable. This may include a focus on being a good listener, keeping a conversation going, and maintaining eye contact. For the man who feels uncomfortable with his ability to arouse a woman, the therapist also may suggest various sexual techniques. In addition, the therapist may help a man who is uncomfortable about making requests to become more assertive in getting his sexual needs met, and to ask a partner about her sexual preferences.

If the premature ejaculation seems to be maintained by relationship problems, the therapist focuses on them. For some men, the sex problem is a manifestation of a power struggle in the relationship. For instance, the man may perceive his partner to be very domineering and as always wanting things her own way. He may not feel comfortable enough to assert himself in the relationship but he remains angry at her nonetheless. If he knows that obtaining sexual satisfaction is important to her, he may not make any effort to delay his ejaculation. In this way, he retaliates for her dominating the relationship in general. In one of our cases, the man's partner felt so insecure about his commitment to her that she encouraged him to ejaculate quickly as a sign that he was still attracted to her. This case is discussed below.

> Bobby and Melissa, a couple in their 30s, had been married for five years. In general, they thought they were reasonably close for the first two years but then the relationship changed. Bobby's job as a trial lawyer often required him to stay late at the office and sometimes he had to work weekends. Even when he was home, he was very preoccupied with his cases. Melissa had a boring part-time job and spent the rest of the week taking care of their eight-month-old son. They lived in a very isolated setting, which made her very dependent upon Bobby's attention to her when he was home. Melissa was jealous because Bobby enjoyed his job. She also began to get very angry at him because Bobby enjoyed playing sports with his male friends on the weekends. She felt that he was less interested in her because he was never at home. In the early years of their marriage, they had had sex on the average of four times per week. Lately, Bobby rarely initiated sex, claiming that he was too tired. Melissa began to think that Bobby was having an affair. She began to initiate sex to see if he was still interested in her. One night Bobby was able to get an erection but he was not sufficiently aroused to ejaculate. Melissa promptly accused him of having an affair with one of the girls at the office, which Bobby denied. Melissa told Bobby that she got the impression that he was having an affair because he was not able to ejaculate; she considered his ejaculation as a sign that he was sexually aroused by her. Because Bobby did not want to make Melissa feel that he was having an affair, from then on he made every effort to ejaculate as soon as intercourse began. After a while, Bobby made no effort to please Melissa but acted as if he just wanted to get the experience over with. They sought treatment when he complained that sex was boring.

The treatment of this couple began with a focus on the relationship. The therapist helped each partner to understand the other's concerns. This meant helping Melissa to understand the pressure that Bobby was experiencing on his job and his needs for achievement, and helping Bobby to understand Melissa's need for meaningful contact with him. Bobby wished that Melissa would be more supportive but recognized that this was difficult when he wasn't home very much. He said that he no longer felt comfortable in having sex because he felt such a great deal of pressure to hurry his ejaculation. The therapist pointed out that Bobby's need to reassure Melissa of his commitment, and Melissa's misconception that rapid ejaculation was a sign of his commitment, had contributed to the premature ejaculation problem.

The therapist then explored some ways to make each partner feel that the other was committed to the relationship. Melissa remarked that she would like to talk to Bobby on the phone each day. In the past, however, he often was very short and didn't really seem interested in talking to her. Bobby agreed to call Melissa two or more times each day when he was free. He requested that Melissa act more warmly to him when he came home from work; he also suggested that she give him about a half hour alone so that he could unwind at that time. She agreed to try this approach. The therapist also explained the philosophy of the stop–start method to the couple and gave Bobby an assignment to start on the exercises during the following week. The therapist suggested that the couple should not engage in intercourse until Bobby was able to delay his ejaculation.

After six sessions, the couple reported that they were spending much more time together. Bobby regularly called Melissa from the office, which made her feel that he was thinking about her. Melissa tried to make it more comfortable for Bobby when he came home. As a consequence, Bobby came home earlier and sometimes worked at home during the day. The couple also had decided to take tennis lessons together on weekends so that they could spend more time together. They regularly made appointments for sex about twice per week, and both reported that sex was very pleasurable at those times. Melissa said that she no longer thought that Bobby was having an affair; she now interpreted Bobby's ability to delay ejaculation as an indication that he wanted to spend more time during sex with her and that he wanted to please her.

ERECTION PROBLEMS

Ron and Susan had been married for five years. Until recently, Ron had not had any difficulty in sexual functioning. But in the last six months, his penis often and unpredictably became soft during intercourse. At first Ron laughed it off and told Susan that he probably was having difficulty because he was too tired. Susan accepted this explanation for a while but then, after noticing no improvement, became concerned that something was wrong. She began to feel that she was undesirable and no longer sexually attractive. As an outgrowth of these feelings, she began to initiate sex more frequently. However, this only made Ron feel more pressure to keep his erection. He began to make excuses whenever they went to bed so that he would not disappoint her. One night Susan persuaded him to try again. Unfortunately, Ron did not get even a partial erection. Susan verbalized her frustration by telling Ron that she had not been sexually satisfied for a long time. Ron decided that he had heard enough. He told Susan that he just wasn't interested in sex anymore, and that she should leave him alone.

Formerly, the term *impotence* was used to describe such a problem as Ron's. This term, however, is used much less today because of its negative connotations of powerlessness and inadequacy.

An erection problem has been defined as the inability of a man to obtain and/or maintain an erection sufficient for penetrating a woman's vagina and ejaculating in at least 75% of his attempts.[6] This 75% is an arbitrary percentage, however, since the man, and his partner if he has one, defines when his ability to gain an erection and keep it is a problem. For some men and their partners, it may not matter if the man does not function successfully every time or almost every time. Other men, however, consider their ability to have intercourse a necessity for having any kind of sexual contact; for these men, a frequent inability to function is more of a problem. It would be unusual, if not impossible, for a man to be able to gain an erection whenever either he or his partner desired it. Most males probably have had occasional difficulty in gaining or maintaining an erection, but they do not consider themselves to have a sex problem.

There are differences among men with erection problems. Some have never had a successful intercourse experience; these men typically are able to gain erections and ejaculate from masturbation and/or from oral and manual stimulation with a partner.[7] Others have had at least one successful experience but now have difficulty gaining or maintaining an erection; many of these men have had previous difficulty with premature ejaculation.

Erection problems are quite varied. A man may be able to gain an erection during foreplay but his penis becomes soft when he either anticipates or actually attempts intercourse. A man may be able to insert his penis in the vagina but, after a few thrusts, it becomes soft and slips out of the vagina. A man may get only a partial erection that is not firm enough for penetration. These problems may occur under some circumstances but not others. A man may get an erection easily enough during masturbation but is not able to get one with a partner. Another fairly common pattern is that of the man who can function successfully with one partner but not with another.

A man typically becomes very concerned at the first sign of an erection problem. He may begin to doubt his ability to function. If he has always received highly positive comments about his sexual performance, he may become even more anxious at the thought of being an inadequate lover. He may make frantic efforts to initiate sex with a variety of partners just to see if he has a problem. The pressure that he places upon himself to perform successfully may cause additional failure. Eventually, the man may consider himself so inadequate that he avoids any sexual contact. If he is single, he may stop dating. If he is married, he may make up reasons to avoid having sex with his wife.

Physical factors initially were thought to account for only a minority of erection problems. In recent years, however, estimates are that at least one-third of all cases, especially in elderly men, may be due to physical factors. These include surgical trauma, poor blood circulation to the penis, spinal cord injury, hormonal abnormalities, and neurological disease. Diabetes mellitus may contribute to erection problems in some men, while it may not influence the erections of other men to any appreciable degree.

Various drugs also may cause or contribute to erection problems. These include most antihypertensives, antidepressants, tranquilizers, and various addictive drugs such as alcohol, barbiturates, heroin, and amphetamines.[8]

A man who consistently has difficulties in obtaining an erection under various conditions (i.e., masturbation, sexual stimulation by a partner) should undergo a comprehensive medical examination. This may include blood tests, urinalysis, and an assessment of hormone levels and blood pressure in the penis. Sleep studies often are used to help differentiate between erection problems that are due to physical versus psychological factors. During rapid eye movement (REM) sleep, physically healthy men usually experience an erection. If a man does not, a strong likelihood exists that the erection problem is partially or totally influenced by some physical factors.

Most erection problems are totally or partially maintained by psychological factors. Perhaps the most frequent factor is "performance anxiety,"[9] or anxiety about whether the man will be able to get an erection, maintain it, and satisfy his partner. This type of anxiety can stem from various sources. Novels, magazines, and movies have perpetuated the notion that much of a man's self-worth is determined by his ability to gain an erection whenever a sexual opportunity presents itself.[10] The man also may feel anxious over not being able to respond when his partner attempts to arouse him; he may not be able to relax enough to focus on the sexual stimulation. Some men also experience anxiety feelings in response to conflicts at school, at work, or with the family. The anxiety created by these conflicts may make it difficult for the man to become aroused.

Many erection problems are due to a combination of physical and psychological factors. In former years, it was thought that if an erection problem was due to physical factors, the man would not be able to have erections at all under any circumstances. This all-or-none thinking is now known to be inaccurate; the influence of physical factors on erections can be a matter of degree. If there is a very slight physical influence, the man consistently may be able to gain reasonably firm erections if he does not suffer from any serious psychological problems. Physical factors can have a moderate influence; the man can have partial erections most of the time if no psychological problems are interfering with his ability to function. Or, physical factors can have a very powerful impact; the man might rarely gain an erection regardless of his psychological well-being, the amount of sexual stimulation he is receiving, or whether he really is sexually attracted to his partner.

Treatment

A man whose erection problem is attributed to physical factors may be given prescribed medication or hormonal therapy, or the medication that he is taking may be altered. He may continue to have an erection problem after the physical factors are treated, however, especially if he is not confident in his ability to function. Sometimes the physical factors cannot be treated, such as in the case of a spinal cord injury. Sex therapy may then help the man to adapt to his limitations and to explore new avenues of sexual expression (see Chapter 6). As we discuss later in this chapter, various surgical procedures, such as the implantation of a penile prosthesis, may be recommended for some men.

Sex therapy for erection problems typically is more involved than sex therapy for premature ejaculation. Treatment usually begins with the therapist attempting to understand and isolate the factors that are maintaining the erection problem. The man is asked specific questions about his sexual experiences and his reactions to them. Which aspects of sex foster anxiety? Does he begin to experience anxiety when he starts to kiss his partner, during more extended foreplay activities, or just before attempting penetration? What is he thinking about before and during sex? Is he focused on the stimulation he is receiving? When does he feel most and least aroused? How much control does he feel over what happens during sex?

The therapist also asks the man questions about his past and present sexual relationships. Have his partners always known what he prefers? How concerned is he about pleasing a partner? What time of day does he usually have sex? Who decides this? When does he feel most like having sex? Has he typically attempted sex early in the relationship, such as on the first date, or later?

In addition, the therapist inquires about the man's social relationships with women. If he does not have a partner, how often does he date? Where does he go on his dates? What role does he usually take in his dating relationships? Active? Passive? To what degree? In what circumstances does he feel most in control? Least in control? How does the man typically deal with conflict? What happens when he is angry? How does he show it? How comfortable does he feel with women? How confident is he when he dates? What are the characteristics of the women to whom he is attracted? If he is married, or if he has a steady partner, what is the nature of the interaction in the relationship? Who decides when to do what? How does he feel about the balance of control in the relationship? Does he sometimes feel overwhelmed or does he feel secure in his position? How much does he trust her? Can he share his feelings with her? Does he know how she feels?

Once the therapist obtains answers to these and other questions, treatment typically addresses a number of concerns. For many men, the therapist focuses on correcting misconceptions about male sexual behavior in particular, and sexual functioning in general. The man is educated about some of the factors that contribute to erection problems, such as excessive anxiety, depression, fatigue, and frustration. He is informed that the sexual satisfaction of many women does not necessarily require the man to get an erection, and that many women are able to reach orgasm in a satisfactory manner from manual or oral stimulation alone. The man is told that it is unrealistic for him to put his self-esteem on the line every time he has sex. The therapist also may inform the man about the female sexual anatomy and suggest various sexual techniques to enhance his partner's arousal.[11]

The therapist also attempts to reduce the man's anxiety in response to sexual situations. The man, regardless of whether he has a steady partner, may be assigned various masturbation exercises. For instance, he may be instructed to stroke his penis until it becomes erect, to stop and let it become soft, and then begin stroking it again. This can help the man practice gaining and losing his erection without the threat of embarrassment or disapproval from a partner.[12] After he loses and regains his erection, he is told to fantasize about having sex with a potential partner. Then, he is told to fantasize about losing and regaining his erection during sex with that partner while he is masturbating. This exercise can help a man to maintain his level of arousal even if he is concerned about losing his erection. It also helps the man gain confidence in his ability to regain an erection.

An important goal of therapy is to help the man get his sexual needs met. To achieve this goal, the therapist helps him to identify his unique conditions for having sex, and helps him feel comfortable enough to establish these conditions before he attempts sex.[13] The man is not expected to be able to function successfully with everyone he meets. Rather, he is encouraged to choose a partner with whom he can talk about his feelings and to whom he feels emotionally close. It is suggested that he not choose women whom he merely wants to impress or to "conquer."

For a man without a steady partner, the therapist suggests that he not attempt intercourse on a first date. More specifically, he is told not to put himself in a potential sexual situation, such as his or her apartment; this will reduce the likelihood that he will feel pressure to initiate sex because the woman may expect him to do so. Instead, he is encouraged to go on a "coffee date" or on a similar non-sexual date so he can get to know the woman as a person and decide if he really likes her.[14] Men who feel uncomfortable around women in general may first be given an assignment to establish a nonsexual friendship relationship with the woman. After the man has had practice developing and maintaining such a relationship, he then may be ready to find a more intimate one.

Using role-play exercises, the therapist helps the man practice making requests for what he wants from sex, to be able to initiate sex when he wants to, and also to say no when he does not. He is shown how to give a partner feedback about preferred ways of kissing and touching by making requests such as "I would like you to touch my penis more softly [or firmly]" or "I would like you to stroke my chest while you touch my penis" or "I would like you to kiss me using more of your tongue." Statements such as these increase the likelihood that the man will get the stimulation he needs to gain and keep an erection. If he does not get an erection, however, he may choose the option of asking his partner if he can please her without intercourse, such as from manual or oral stimulation. As another option, the man might suggest to his partner that he is not really that aroused and that it would be better to wait until another time. Or, the man might express his desire to please his partner by making a statement such as "I would enjoy touching you awhile" or "Why don't I touch you in a way that you would like? Show me how you would like to be touched." This option can help the man to feel more comfortable and in control during sex. Furthermore, once the man discovers his partner's sexual preferences, he typically feels less pressure because the guesswork has been removed.

Some men lose their erections when they begin to focus on a partner's pleasure instead of on their own. For these men, the therapist may assign sensate focus exercises.[15] The man's partner strokes his penis until it becomes erect, stops until the erection subsides, and then begins to stimulate his penis again. This "teasing" procedure is repeated several times to help the man feel comfortable losing and then regaining his erection during sexual contact.[16] The couple is told to refrain from sexual intercourse until the man successfully maintains an erect penis when his partner stimulates him either manually or orally. Men who have difficulty feeling comfortable in being touched by a partner while they remain passive are told to stimulate the woman in her preferred manner for an equivalent amount of time, and to do this before they themselves are focused on.

In the next step, the woman stimulates the man until he has a firm erection. Using the woman-on-top position, she then inserts his penis; she lies still until he feels comfortable being inside her vagina, and then she slowly begins to move her hips. This is so the man can experience "nondemand intercourse" or intercourse during which he does not feel pressure to perform. The man then is encouraged to thrust until he ejaculates if desired. In subsequent interactions, the man may be instructed to lose his erection on purpose. The exercise attempts to give the man a sense of voluntary control over gaining an erection.[17]

Often, an important aspect of treatment is a focus on the man's relationship with a partner. This is especially important because a man who is in a relationship marked by stress, conflict, and power struggles often feels too anxious, insecure, inadequate, or angry to gain or keep an erection. This is illustrated in the case below.

Tom, a 32-year-old computer salesman, sought treatment because of an erection problem. For the last year, he typi-

cally gained an erection during foreplay but lost it whenever he attempted intercourse. His 27-year-old wife, Ellen,
began to expect that she would not be sexually fulfilled. As
a consequence, she began to make less of an effort to please
him during foreplay. Tom interpreted Ellen's growing lack
of interest as an indication that he was no longer sexually
desirable. He began to feel a great deal of anxiety whenever
he had sex. Occasionally, when Tom would verbalize a
desire for sex, Ellen would say something like "Only if you
are sure that you can do it." Predictably, this created even
more anxiety for Tom since he began to believe that she
would not be satisfied with anything but a perfect sexual
experience.

Tom also was experiencing a great deal of anxiety from
other sources. In the second year of his marriage, he had
taken a calculated risk and left a fairly high-paying and
secure job to go into a private business. His wife did not
really want him to change jobs but she went along with his
decision. Unfortunately, the business folded after one year,
and Tom was forced to take a job that he didn't really want
as a computer salesman for less pay. His job was quite
stressful since he worked on commission. To make matters
worse, Ellen often reminded him that she was dissatisfied
with his reduced income.

In the first few sessions, the therapist encouraged the
couple to discuss their frustrated and angry feelings about
the events of the last two years. Tom discussed the stress
that he felt from his job and his disappointment about his
reduced financial status. He also got in touch with the
anger that he felt toward Ellen because she was not being
supportive. Ellen's feelings of dissatisfaction and hostility
toward Tom also were addressed. For a long time she had
resented his decision to change jobs but she didn't feel that
it was her place to really oppose the decision at first. She
admitted that she probably was taking her frustrations
about Tom's involvement with his job out on their sex life.
Both partners began to realize that they hadn't really com-

municated their underlying feelings of hurt and frustration. They verbalized a strong commitment to work on the
relationship.

In the third session, Tom felt comfortable enough to
share his fear of sexual failure with Ellen; this helped her
to understand how some of her hostile comments about his
erection problem had affected him. Ellen said that she
really had liked sex with Tom in the past and she wanted
to improve their sex life. The therapist suggested that Tom
might be in a better mood after work if he had time to relax
and unwind from the job-related pressure. Tom agreed and
requested that Ellen give him about an hour reading the
paper to get settled. The therapist also focused on helping
Ellen to feel more comfortable in expressing her needs and
ideas to Tom in a way that reduced the likelihood that he
would feel threatened.

The couple began the next session stating that they
were now ready for a more specific focus on the sexual
relationship. They were asked to discuss their preferences
for specific sexual behaviors and their ideal sexual interactions. Subsequently, they were given an assignment to
participate in nongenital touching with verbal feedback.
Since they were going to be out of town for two weeks,
they were encouraged to add genital touching to this exercise if all went well. Tom had no difficulty getting an erection and keeping it during these exercises; nevertheless,
they did not attempt intercourse because of the therapist's
suggestion that they wait. They said that they were ready
to go ahead with intercourse and the therapist concurred.

In the last session, the sixth, Tom reported that he had
had no difficulty in gaining an erection and keeping it during sex. He thought that the idea of making appointments
for sex was very helpful since he felt confident that Ellen
would be interested in sex at those times; before treatment,
the guesswork involved in determining whether she was

interested and how she would react to him had made sex an extremely pressure-packed situation. The partners were spending much more time together and they were much more satisfied with the relationship in general. Tom additionally reported that he was feeling much more capable of handling the pressure from work since he felt closer to Ellen.

The Option of a Penile Prosthesis

Some erection problems, such as those that occur for men with spinal injury, are irreversible. In these cases, the surgical implantation of a penile prosthesis is an option.

Two types of penile prostheses are the most common. One type results in a permanent erection; an incision is made in the penis or just behind the scrotum. A semirigid, silicone rod then is inserted into each of the corpora cavernosa. Sometimes, only one rod is implanted between the two corpora cavernosa. The prosthesis costs about $3500, including hospitalization.

The second type is the inflatable or hydraulic prosthesis. When it is inserted, an incision is made in the abdomen or the scrotum. The surgeon then places two expandable balloonlike cylinders into the corpora cavernosa. When the man presses a particular spot on the scrotum, he can gain and lose his erection. The cost of the inflatable prosthesis is about $1800, in addition to hospitalization; sometimes the total expense can be $8000.

The inflatable prosthesis produces an erection that approximates a normal one more closely than does the silicone rod prosthesis; however, the former is more likely to develop mechanical problems. There is a slight risk of infection associated with the implantation of the silicone rod prosthesis, and surgical removal due to complications occurs much more frequently than with the inflatable device.[18] It should be noted that many medical insurance programs do not cover the cost of surgery for either prosthesis.

Some men who have had an erection problem for a long time expect that a prosthesis will solve all their sex and relationship problems. Because this expectation is unrealistic, many surgeons refer a man who desires a penile prosthesis to a sex therapist before agreeing to implant one. Such a referral serves two purposes. The first is to determine whether sex therapy might foster improvement in the man's sexual functioning to the point that he and his partner are satisfied. If this were to happen, the man would not have to spend the money for the prosthesis. The second purpose is to determine why the man wants a prosthesis. Is it his idea or his partner's? What was his sexual functioning before his erection problem? What have his sexual experiences been like since that time? Have the man and his partner tried ways other than intercourse to have sex, such as mutual manual stimulation or oral sex? It also is considered important that the man's partner, if he has one, be involved in the decision to implant the prosthesis. Some partners worry that they may get an injury from the implant or that intercourse might hurt the penis. Some partners are concerned that the man will leave the relationship once he can function sexually (sometimes this happens). A partner who is not in favor of the prosthesis likely will not help the man's adjustment to it.

Overall, most men who have a penile prosthesis seem to be quite satisfied. Even men who are disappointed with their prosthesis-induced erection rarely ask to have it removed.

Other Surgical Procedures

Two other surgical procedures for physically based erection problems are still in the early stages of development. One procedure, known as penile revascularization surgery, has been used with men who have restricted blood flow to the penis. In these cases, diagnostic tests establish that there is a block in the arteries that normally supply blood to the penis. Since the penis becomes erect from increasing blood supply, a block in blood flow can cause an erection problem. Surgery attempts to restore normal blood flow to the penis by artificially connecting two arteries. This procedure is not always successful. A major complication is that the new arterial connection often closes up soon after surgery; priapism (painful erection) also has occurred. When the surgery is successful, the man can gain erections and resume normal sexual activity. Some couples may prefer this type of surgery over implanting a penile prosthesis because it does not involve placing any kind of "unnatural device" inside the penis. Arterial surgery, while still in need of refinement, does seem to offer promise as an alternative treatment for some men with erection problems.[19]

A second type of surgical procedure appears promising. Some men have abnormal drainage from the spongy bodies, known as the corpora cavernosa, in the penile shaft. When diagnostic tests can identify the specific area that is leaking, it can be stitched up surgically. This is a relatively simple operation to correct erectile failure, but it is useful only in certain cases.

EJACULATORY INHIBITION

Don and Cathy had been dating for eight months. They spent a lot of time together and they enjoyed each other's company. But, sex was a problem. It was not that Don ejaculated too soon, or that he was unable to gain an erection. The problem was that Don rarely ejaculated during intercourse. As a consequence, Cathy often felt as if Don was not really interested in having sex with her. Don realized that part of the problem was that it was difficult for him to pay attention to what was going on. During intercourse, he often started thinking about an unfinished assignment at work or what he and Cathy were going to do the next day. In an effort to become more aroused, he even tried thinking about some particularly erotic scenes from an X-rated movie that he had seen last year. While these thoughts seemed to increase his arousal level, it still was difficult for him to "get over the brink." When Cathy finally asked him about why he could get an erection easily enough but often not ejaculate, he didn't have any answers. Cathy also told him that she was becoming less interested in having sex with him because she often experienced considerable soreness in her vagina when intercourse lasted for 25 minutes or longer. Don felt even more frustrated after this talk, especially since intercourse was equally unsatisfying for him. He got mad at himself for making attempts to please Cathy while he never felt sexually satisfied himself.

Men with ejaculatory inhibition (also known as *retarded ejaculation*, but this term has negative connotations) have difficulty ejaculating even when receiving sexual stimulation. Some of these men can ejaculate from masturbation or from other nonintercourse sexual activities, but not during intercourse. Like Don, many become aroused sufficiently to gain an erection, but it is very difficult for them to reach the necessary level of arousal for ejaculation. When they do ejaculate, it usually is under conditions of receiving sexual stimulation for long periods of time; this often is very frustrating for both the man and his partner. The most severe form of ejaculatory inhibition is when the man is unable to ejaculate from any type of sexual stimulation, including masturbation.

Ejaculatory inhibition is quite rare. Thus, not much is really known about the factors that maintain this problem. The physical factors seem to include diabetes, various drugs, and various neurological diseases that influence the part of the nervous system controlling the ejaculatory response.

A number of psychological factors are thought to influence ejaculatory inhibition. One is anxiety. The man may be anxious about the possibility that he will disappoint his partner, that she will think he is awkward in his approach, or that she will consider him to be unmasculine. It is as if the man is not really involved during the experience; he considers sex to be a performance task for the purpose of fostering his partner's orgasm. Much of this way of thinking and behaving is tied to our culture's unrealistic expectations of male sexual performance. Men are expected to delay ejaculating for a certain undefined amount of time until they believe a partner is satisfied. The man may believe that the longer he lasts, the greater the probability that his partner will be satisfied.[20] A man who believes that his masculinity is positively influenced by the number of times that a partner reaches orgasm may try to prolong intercourse indefinitely for this purpose. He may become so adept at delaying his ejaculation, however, that it then becomes difficult for him to ejaculate when he wants to. He also may be too tired to continue thrusting, or his partner is either too tired or not interested in stimulating him after she reaches orgasm. Also, the man may not realize that many women do not desire or need an extended period of time in intercourse to be sexually satisfied. On the contrary, some women become sore and uncomfortable after having intercourse for 20 minutes or longer, and some have reached one or more orgasms by that time.

Some sex therapists, such as Bernie Apfelbaum,[21] believe that ejaculatory inhibition is maintained, at least in part, by a desire or arousal problem (these are discussed in Chapter 5). Even though the man typically can gain an erection quite easily in sexual situations, he often is not really interested. Some do not even like to have erections. Some may consider intercourse to be a traumatic or unpleasant event. Thus, the erection of the man with ejaculatory inhibition is not necessarily a sign of subjective arousal.

Cultural messages about what sex should be like for males can influence ejaculatory inhibition in other ways. A man is not expected to need extended pleasuring to become aroused; he should be able to get turned on without any help from his partner. This unrealistic way of thinking has made it very difficult and even embarrassing for some men to request, for example, that a partner kiss in a different way, stroke the chest in a certain manner, or move in a preferred motion during intercourse.

The ejaculatory inhibition of some men seems to be attributed to relationship problems. A man may not trust his partner or really feel emotionally close to her. Rather, he may harbor hostile feelings that interfere with his ability to feel comfortable during sex. He may find it difficult to become sufficiently aroused to ejaculate, and he may even blame his partner for not being able to satisfy him. If she considers his ejaculation to be a sign that he is satisfied, he may delay his ejaculation as an indirect expression of his angry feelings. Typically, this pattern results in neither partner being sexually satisfied.

Treatment

The therapist begins treatment by asking questions about the man's sexual behavior and his reactions to the problem. Under which, if any, circumstances does he ejaculate? Masturbation? Foreplay? Intercourse? When is he most or least aroused? What is he thinking and feeling during sex play? What is he thinking and feeling when he wants to ejaculate and he does not? What are his partner's reactions at these times?

Once the therapist understands the factors that seem to be maintaining the man's ejaculatory inhibition, treatment is focused on these factors. For men who seem to have an excessive need to please a partner, the therapist might assign Zilbergeld's *Male Sexuality*[22] as homework. The client's reactions to this book are discussed to help him better understand the negative influence of unrealistic stereotypes on his perception of his role in sex. Also, the therapist might highlight the importance of the man asking his partner about the type of stimulation she prefers so that he can feel more confident in knowing what she likes. The therapist may help the man feel more comfortable in getting this information by role-playing methods.

Treatment is focused on helping the man reach higher levels of sexual arousal. If he becomes more aroused when his partner strokes his buttocks, he is encouraged to ask his partner to do so, and to take her hand and guide it in the preferred manner. The therapist also stresses the importance of the man focusing on what it feels like as his partner touches his body. He also is told to focus on the pleasurable sensations from his penis being in the vagina. The therapist may suggest that the man increase the speed of his thrusting.[23] He is encouraged to focus on the most arousing aspects of his partner's body. For instance, if he is most aroused from looking at or touching his partner's breasts, he is encouraged to focus on what they look and feel like.

If a couple is being treated, the therapist often offers some suggestions for the woman as well. If the man becomes more aroused whenever his partner is more active or verbally expressive during sex, the therapist may suggest that she do so more often and more intensely than usual. The man can focus on her mounting arousal as a way to enhance his own arousal. The therapist also may suggest that the couple try different manual or oral sexual techniques, and different intercourse positions. From these exercises, both partners may discover new and more exciting ways to give and receive stimulation. Some sex therapists, such as Barry McCarthy,[24] encourage both partners to stimulate each other in a preferred manner during intercourse. The man is told to give his partner feedback about his mounting arousal as well as to request further stimulation when it is desired. These exercises were helpful in the case below.

> Ed, a 23-year-old college student, entered treatment because his 21-year-old girl friend, Denise, had told him that she couldn't understand why he couldn't ejaculate. Although it was very easy for him to get erections in a sexual situation, he had ejaculated during intercourse with prior partners only on rare occasions; he had never done so with Denise. Ed said that he rarely masturbated but almost always ejaculated when he did. He told the therapist that he felt somewhat aroused during sex but he always was very aware of outside sounds during sex play; this made it difficult for him to really let himself go. Furthermore, while he acknowledged that Denise was very attractive, it bothered him that she sometimes would not shower and wash her hair before sex. Usually, she claimed that she was just too tired from her job as a waitress. Ed, who had never smoked, also said that the smoke that lingered in Denise's hair after work was a definite turn-off. He knew that he should tell Denise of these concerns but he had just not been able to do so. When asked to describe his most arousing sexual interaction, Ed gave an account of an experience that he had had two years earlier. While on a week-long vacation, he had met a woman who was very attractive. When they eventually had sex, she touched him in a very soft and sensual manner, and she also told him what it was like when he was touching her. She described what she

was doing to him and she wanted him to talk to her in the same way. Ed also said that she stroked his buttocks in a certain manner and occasionally would put a finger in his anus when he was close to reaching ejaculation. All of these aspects of his sexual interaction with this woman really excited Ed, and he had never had any difficulty ejaculating with her. Nevertheless, he just didn't feel comfortable in communicating this information to Denise.

Treatment initially focused on identifying the aspects of foreplay and intercourse that Ed found most arousing in his interactions with Denise. The therapist suggested that it would be important to include Denise in subsequent sessions. In the next session, which both partners attended, the therapist recommended that each give the other feedback during sex about what it felt like when being touched. Both partners were encouraged to express their reactions during sex in the form of increased breathing, sighs, and moans. Each partner was encouraged to ask the other what was being felt so that both could focus on the ongoing experience. Ed was told to "really feel" the contours of Denise's body that he found most arousing. In addition, the couple was encouraged to communicate during sex by guiding each other in preferred stroking motions. The therapist also recommended that the couple should take a shower or bath together before sex so that both would feel more relaxed and comfortable.

After four sessions, Ed reported that he was not as easily distracted during sex and that he was able to focus on the experience practically all of the time. He said that he was able to ejaculate within 15 minutes of penetration about 90% of the time; this outcome was quite acceptable to both. They agreed that they enjoyed foreplay activities more than before, and that there was less pressure to have intercourse. In fact, Denise revealed that she often enjoyed manually stroking Ed until he ejaculated. Denise also said that Ed had become much more open in sharing his feelings since treatment had begun.

Men with ejaculatory inhibition who do not have a partner may be trained in relaxation and then guided through a sequence of sexual fantasies. The man may be asked to imagine ejaculating while he is stimulating himself, then to imagine ejaculating during nonintercourse activities with a partner, and finally to imagine ejaculating during intercourse itself.

If the man can reach ejaculation only during masturbation, and he has a partner, the therapist may encourage the man to masturbate to ejaculation with his partner present. Then, the woman is instructed to gradually manually stimulate his penis until he ejaculates. Subsequently, the woman manually stimulates his penis until he is close to ejaculation; at this point, she inserts his penis into her vagina. If the man does not ejaculate, he withdraws his penis, and the woman begins stimulating him again. This procedure is repeated until the man ejaculates inside the vagina. Then, the couple is instructed to attempt intercourse earlier in the sequence until the man is able to ejaculate from penile thrusting without being dependent upon the extended manual stimulation from his partner.

Couples in which the man has less difficulty in ejaculating during intercourse may be instructed to engage in prolonged foreplay activities until both partners are highly aroused. Then, they are encouraged to begin intercourse until the man begins to lose his arousal, or until one or both partners become tired. At this point, the woman manually or orally stimulates his penis or any other part of his body that is arousing to the man. When the man again feels highly aroused, intercourse is resumed. This technique, which is designed to foster more relaxed sexual interactions and reduce the performance demands on both partners, may be used more than once during a given sexual interaction until the man ejaculates inside the vagina. Of course, this technique contradicts the notion that intercourse, once it begins, must proceed until the man ejaculates. A further advantage is that brief rests during intercourse also may enhance the woman's pleasure.

If the ejaculatory inhibition is being maintained by relationship problems, the therapist also may focus on the couple's characteristic way of dealing with each other. This may include helping both partners to develop a closer, more positive relationship. The therapist may encourage both partners to spend more time together and to talk more openly about personal feelings toward each other and toward life in general. If the man tends to keep feelings such as anger, fear, anxiety, joy, and happiness inside, he is encouraged to verbalize these feelings when they arise. With practice, the man may begin to feel more comfortable about sharing these feelings. His ability to do so may facilitate a feeling of greater emotional closeness; this may reduce his need for being in control during sex. When the man's ejaculatory inhibition can be attributed to unsettled conflicts in the relationship, the therapist helps the couple to deal with these conflicts in a way that defuses the anger that is felt by both partners.

REFERENCES

1. W. H. Masters, V. E. Johnson, *Human Sexual Inadequacy* (Boston: Little, Brown, 1970).
2. J. H. Semans, "Premature Ejaculation: A New Approach," *Southern Medical Journal* (49) (1956), pp. 353–358.
3. B. Zilbergeld, *Male Sexuality: A Guide to Sexual Fulfillment* (Boston: Little, Brown, 1978).
4. Masters, Johnson, 1970.
5. J. LoPiccolo, "Direct Treatment of Sexual Dysfunction," in *Handbook of Sex Therapy*, ed. J. LoPiccolo and L. LoPiccolo (New York: Plenum, 1978).

6. P. R. Kilmann, R. R. Auerbach, "Treatment of Premature Ejaculation and Psychogenic Impotence: A Critical Review of the Literature," *Archives of Sexual Behavior* 8 (1979), pp. 81–100.
7. B. W. McCarthy, "Treatment of Secondary Erectile Dysfunction in Males Without Partners," *Journal of Sex Education and Therapy* 6 (1980), pp. 29–34.
8. J. Reckless, N. Geiger, "Impotence as a Practical Problem," in *Handbook of Sex Therapy*, ed. J. LoPiccolo and L. LoPiccolo (New York: Plenum, 1978).
9. Masters, Johnson, 1970.
10. Zilbergeld, 1978.
11. McCarthy, 1980.
12. Ibid.
13. Zilbergeld, 1978.
14. Ibid.
15. Masters, Johnson, 1970.
16. Zilbergeld, 1978.
17. Ibid.
18. W. M. Sotile, "The Penile Prosthesis: A Review," *Journal of Sex and Marital Therapy* 5 (1979), pp. 90–102.
19. G. Wagner, "Penile Dysfunctions Due to Local Disorders," in *Impotence: Physiological, Psychological, Surgical Diagnosis and Treatment*, ed. G. Wagner and R. Green (New York: Plenum Press, 1981).
20. Zilbergeld, 1978.
21. B. Apfelbaum, "The Diagnosis and Treatment of Retarded Ejaculation," in *Principles and Practice of Sex Therapy*, ed. S. R. Leiblum and L. A. Pervin (New York: Guilford Press, 1980).
22. Zilbergeld, 1978.
23. B. W. McCarthy, "Strategies and Techniques for the Treatment of Ejaculatory Inhibition," *Journal of Sex Education and Therapy* 7 (1981), pp. 20–23.
24. Ibid.

Chapter Four

FEMALE SEXUAL PROBLEMS

In former years, many people of both sexes did not consider women to be sexual beings. Women were expected to inhibit their sexuality. Sex was something that a woman was expected to engage in not to obtain pleasure for herself but merely to please her partner. Today, however, much of this thinking has changed. The sexual liberation movement has helped many women to acknowledge their sexual feelings. Women are being told that they have the capacity for, and indeed the right to, sexual satisfaction and orgasms, even multiple orgasms. While this more liberal way of thinking has helped many women become more sexually satisfied, many others still experience difficulties in sexual functioning. In this chapter, we discuss orgasm problems, vaginismus, and painful intercourse.

ORGASM PROBLEMS

Susan, a 24-year-old unmarried secretary, practically always reached orgasm after about three minutes of masturbation. However, she had never reached orgasm from foreplay or from intercourse. With her current boyfriend, Bill, a 28-year-old lawyer, she would get turned on to a certain point but could not reach a higher level of arousal. Susan knew that at least part of the reason for her inability to reach orgasm was that she did not feel comfortable enough telling him the specific way that she would like him to touch her clitoris (she had learned this from masturbation). It also was difficult for her to relax during sex because he was not very gentle when he touched her breasts. She was fairly certain that Bill would be offended if she wanted him to change his touching manner, and that he would doubt his ability to be a good lover. A further distraction during sex was that Susan often wondered whether Bill really found her body attractive; she always worried that he might be comparing her body to those of his former girl friends. Bill could tell that Susan was not really involved in sex. Sometimes, just before he initiated, he would comment that he wished she would be more responsive. At those times, Susan would become so concerned about possibly disappointing him that she had even more difficulty relaxing. As a consequence, she began to fake orgasms. For a while, this made Bill feel more assured about his ability to arouse her. But, after about one month, Bill again remarked that Susan did not seem to like sex. One night, after an argument, Bill called her "unresponsive" and "frigid" in comparison with other women. This made Susan very angry, and during a temper tantrum, she told him that she had never had an orgasm with him, and that she had been faking it just so he would feel good about himself. First, Bill blamed himself for not being able to satisfy Susan. Then, he got very mad at her. He said that he was not going to see her anymore and that he was going to start looking for a partner who enjoyed sex as much as he did.

The inability to reach orgasm, or to do it consistently, is the most common female sexual problem. When does a woman have an orgasm problem? There is no absolute criterion. Women differ in their expectations for reaching orgasm. Some want to reach orgasm every time they have sex. Others are not so concerned about reaching orgasm each time but are satisfied if they reach a certain arousal level, or if they feel emotionally close to a partner during sex. We can say that an orgasm problem exists when a woman is dissatisfied with her ability to reach orgasm, regardless of the frequency.

Women who seek treatment for an orgasm problem report a variety of difficulties. Some have never reached orgasm by any means with or without a partner. Like the case of Susan above, some reach orgasm from masturbation but not with a partner. Some reach orgasm when a partner stimulates them manually or orally but not from intercourse alone. Others reach orgasm during intercourse only if the clitoris is being manually stimulated at the same time, either by themselves or by a partner. This is considered a normal variation, even though many women want to reach orgasm through intercourse without the concurrent manual stimulation of the clitoris. Others have reached orgasm at least once in their lives but now do so very infrequently.

Women who report an orgasm problem also show different patterns of sexual arousal in response to sexual stimulation. Some do not become aroused even minimally, no matter how much stimulation they receive. Others initially experience mild arousal but do not seem to be able to increase it. Others reach a very high level of arousal fairly quickly but seem unable to "get over the brink." Still others cannot maintain a high arousal level long enough to reach orgasm; their arousal level may fluctuate in an unpredictable fashion.[1]

What factors contribute to orgasm problems? The influence of physical factors seems to be uncommon, although we really don't know much about this. An orgasm problem may occur from clitoral adhesions, a condition that exists when the hood of the clitoris is attached to the shaft; this may inhibit the clitoris from retracting during sexual stimulation. Very weak vaginal muscles also may decrease a woman's potential for reaching orgasm. Other physical factors that may contribute to orgasm problems, such as spinal cord injuries, are discussed in Chapter 6.

The great majority of orgasm problems are maintained by one or more psychological factors. Perhaps the most common factor is the repression of female sexuality, which has existed in our culture for many years and, though to a lesser degree, continues to exist today. As a consequence, many women believe that they should inhibit their sexual impulses, reject men's advances, and refrain from sexual intimacy until they are in a committed relationship. Although many women endorse the more modern notion of male/female equality, many have been so accustomed to keeping their sexual feelings under wraps for so many years that it is difficult for them to unshackle their sexual inhibitions. This task is made even more difficult by the reality that many men don't respect women if they do not resist their advances at least somewhat.

Some women with an orgasm problem were raised in a home in which sex was never discussed in a positive light, if at all. Men may have been described as "only interested in sex" or "only out for themselves." The woman may have been told not to expect any satisfaction for herself. Other women had a very strong religious upbringing in which premarital sex was strongly disapproved of. Even after marriage, they still have difficulty "letting go." Still other women had very negative sexual experiences with men. They may have been forced to have sex on a date, or by a stranger. As a consequence, the woman may not realize that sex can be a pleasurable experience. Instead, she believes that it is an activity to be tolerated or avoided. This way of thinking makes it very difficult for a woman to let herself become aroused.

The impact of the sexual liberation movement certainly has reduced the sexual inhibitions of many women, but, at the same time, it has generated a considerable degree of anxiety. In years past, the guidelines for acceptable and appropriate female sexual behavior were fairly clearly defined. Sex was considered the man's responsibility and the woman was not supposed to know much about how to please him. The woman often was a passive recipient rather than the taker of an active role. Today, the woman who does not consider sex to hold a fairly high priority in a relationship is not considered desirable by many men. Some men now expect women to be interested in having sex at a high frequency, to be proficient in various sexual techniques such as oral sex, to feel comfortable initiating sex, and to be interested in experimenting with new variations. Even though it is unrealistic to expect that women who have spent much of their lives denying their sexual feelings should enjoy sex and participate with complete abandon, many men want a "sexually liberated" woman. These modern-day expectations that some men (and women) have for female sexual behavior have created a type of performance anxiety in many women.

The orgasm problems of some women are attributed to the woman's anxiety over losing conscious control over her feelings during orgasm. Orgasm can be a very intense experience, resulting in a flood of emotion as well as a loss of voluntary control over body movements. This release of physical and emotional tension is, of course, largely what makes an orgasm so pleasurable. Yet many women are afraid to let themselves go and experience these intense feelings. Some may be unfamiliar with their capacity for sexual arousal and satisfaction. The woman may not have explored the parts of her body that are most sensitive to touch, or the type of stroking and caressing that offers the most pleasure. Some women feel guilt about their ability to become aroused, especially if they have never considered themselves as sexual beings. Some fear that at the point of orgasm they will lose consciousness, urinate, and perhaps not act "ladylike"; they are concerned that a partner may not react with favor to moans or exaggerated physical movements, which they need to facilitate their arousal level. Some women may fear that letting go of their feelings enough so that their partner can bring them to orgasm might make them too emotionally vulnerable. A woman who has difficulty trusting men in general may not want to give a partner that much control over her. A woman may not really want to have sex but does so because she feels obligated; she may be unable to get aroused because she is mad at herself for giving in.

Some women with an orgasm problem have difficulty focusing on sexual stimulation. They may be easily distracted by external events during sex. For example, they may be unable to become aroused if they hear the children playing in the next room, a neighbor talking, or a dog barking. While a partner attempts to arouse them, they may be preoccupied with other interfering thoughts. Does he find me attractive? Is he only touching me for his benefit? Does he really care about me? If I let myself go, will he think of me as "wild and free"? Other women have difficulty concentrating because they feel obligated to respond to a partner's initiations even though they really don't want to have sex at that time; a woman may wish that she were somewhere else or with someone else.

Some orgasm problems can be attributed to the sexual functioning of the woman's partner. Some men are very awkward lovers and just want to please themselves. They are unaware that a partner might prefer a considerable amount of time in kissing and entire-body caressing in a slow, sensual manner before intercourse. Some men are unfamiliar with the location of the clitoris and the importance of its stimulation for most women. Some men believe that any vaginal lubrication at all is a sign that the woman is ready and willing to have intercourse. Some men typically ejaculate soon after penetration and some lose their erection shortly after penetration. Some men are very receptive to a woman requesting specific types of stimulation, while others resent the implication that they are not good lovers. In some cases, the man who believes that he is the "sexual expert" may continue to stimulate the woman the way that *he* prefers without modifying his approach in accordance with her feedback. A woman whose partner exhibits one or more of these characteristics may not receive a sufficient degree of stimulation to reach orgasm.

A woman's unwillingness or inability to communicate her preferences for specific types of sexual stimulation to a partner also can contribute to an orgasm problem. She may refrain from giving this information to a partner because, if she does, he may believe that she is "oversexed" or that she has had too much experience with previous partners.

Many orgasm problems are due, at least in part, to relationship problems. A woman in a relationship that is not emotionally satisfying may experience difficulty with physical intimacy. It may be difficult for her to give in to sexual feelings if she doubts her partner's commitment. If she is angry at her partner, it may be even more difficult for her to respond.

Treatment

As a first step, the therapist usually asks the woman about her orgasm problem and how it is manifested. Has she ever reached orgasm before? If not, how aroused does she actually get? What does it feel like to be sexually stimulated? What is she thinking about when this is happening? What would an orgasm be like for her? In which situations does she get most aroused? Least aroused? What does she think inhibits her from becoming even more aroused?

If a woman has reached orgasm at least once in the past, the therapist asks other questions. For example, what was going on when she reached orgasm in contrast to when she didn't? What type of stimulation was she receiving? What were the circumstances surrounding these times? What time of the day? What events had occurred immediately prior to the sexual interaction? Who initiated sex? What type of stimulation was she receiving? What was she thinking about when she was being stimulated? What did it feel like?

If the woman has a partner, the therapist may ask specific questions about the sexual and nonsexual relationship. Who usually initiates sex? How comfortable is it for her to refuse when she is not interested? Does her partner know what pleases her sexually? Has she actually told him what she likes? Is she overly concerned about pleasing him? Is it difficult for her to relax unless she is attempting to please him? How does she feel about the relationship? How does he know when she is angry? Does the couple resolve conflicts or is the relationship characterized by many unsettled issues? If so, which ones? How committed is she to the relationship? What is her partner's commitment? Does her partner have any problem with delaying his ejaculation? Is the duration of intercourse satisfactory for her? Does her partner have any difficulty getting and keeping his erection? How does she feel after sex?

Once the therapist understands the factors that may be blocking the woman from reaching orgasm, the treatment plan is formulated. Typically, treatment differs somewhat for the woman who has never reached orgasm in contrast to the woman who reaches orgasm at a less than desirable rate. To help the woman who has never reached orgasm, the therapist usually tells her that she is most likely to do so from masturbation. Some women feel uncomfortable with the idea of touching themselves for the purpose of sexual arousal; the therapist may inform the woman that many women masturbate. She may be told that an advantage of using masturbation is to discover her unique conditions for maximum sexual arousal, and that she does not have to worry about pleasing a partner. The therapist also may discuss the negative impact of our culture's traditional views of female sexuality on female sexual arousal. The woman may be encouraged to be more selfish about becoming sexually aroused. The therapist may assign Shere Hite's *The Hite Report*[2] as homework so that the woman can learn about different masturbation techniques. The therapist also may assign other reading materials, such as Lonnie Barbach's *For Yourself*[3] or *For Each Other: Sharing Sexual Intimacy*,[4] to highlight the notion that women have the right and the capability to experience sexual pleasure.

Many therapists use some modification of the masturbation program published by Joseph LoPiccolo and W. C. Lobitz in 1972.[5] Initially, the woman may be given an assignment to focus on a favorite sexual fantasy for a designated time each day for at least a half hour. Subsequently, the woman might be asked to choose a time and a place free from outside distractions and to begin touching herself in any way that she would like while she concentrates on the sexual fantasy; she is told to take the phone off the hook to make sure that she will not be disturbed. The woman is asked to touch herself to "see what happens" without worrying about whether she will reach orgasm. If she does not, she may be encouraged to use a vibrator for this purpose.

Once orgasm is reached, the woman with a partner is encouraged to masturbate in his presence. From this procedure, her partner can discover how she enjoys touching herself. He then can attempt to stimulate her in a like manner, while she guides him and gives him feedback. This is done by moving his hand in the desired stroking motion and by making positive comments when he is stroking her in a pleasing manner (i.e., "That feels good," "I really like that," "Please don't stop"). Subsequently, the couple is encouraged to have intercourse while the man or the woman manually stimulates her clitoris.

Sometimes the group method is used to treat women who have difficulty reaching orgasm. These groups, initially popularized by sex therapist Lonnie Barbach,[6] typically have the implicit goal of helping the woman to reach orgasm from masturbation and then with a partner if desired. Other goals include helping the woman to become familiar and comfortable with her body, to label and express her arousal more freely, to identify her sexual needs, and to express them to a partner.[7] Typically, about seven or eight women meet in a group with a female therapist. Topics such as what the women first learned about sex, what sex has meant to them, and their goals for positive sexual functioning are discussed. Clinical observations suggest that these groups provide considerable support and encouragement in helping the women to understand more about their sexuality and how to meet their sexual needs.

Helping a woman to reach orgasm during intercourse seems to be one of the most difficult therapeutic tasks. Some therapists believe that the ability of a woman to reach orgasm during intercourse is related to at least two factors: the woman's sensitivity to internal stimulation— that is, stimulation inside the vagina—and to high levels of sexual arousal. Both of these factors can be learned, at least to some extent.[8] Other therapists have suggested that the nerves inside the vagina are relatively insensitive, and they cite this as the reason for a treatment focus on getting the woman to receive more extended foreplay.[9] These therapists attempt to show the woman how to concentrate on sexual stimulation, how to relax sufficiently to counteract any feelings of anxiety, and, at the same time, how to tell and show her partner the ways that she would like to be touched. For some women, however, reaching orgasm from intercourse does not seem to have anything to do with receiving more arousing foreplay for a longer period of time. Instead, the experience of intercourse itself determines whether the woman reaches orgasm. It appears that differences exist among women in the type and sequence of sexual stimulation necessary to reach orgasm.

Some women have reached orgasm sometime in the past but now have difficulty. If a couple is being treated, the therapist typically includes a more extended focus on sexual and communication techniques. The therapist restructures the sexual interaction so that both partners are more sensitive to each other's sexual needs. Sometimes, this merely involves a focus on each partner verbalizing sexual preferences to the other. In some cases, the focus may be on helping the man to become more sensitive to the woman's needs for extended foreplay, and for concurrent clitoral stimulation during intercourse. The therapist also may focus on broader relationship problems that are interfering with the couple's, and particularly the woman's, sexual satisfaction. Some women are unable to reach orgasm during sex, at least in part, because of angry feelings. This is shown in the following case.

> Laurie, a 25-year-old housewife and mother, entered treatment with her husband, John, a 30-year-old accountant. Laurie had been able to reach orgasm the few times that she had masturbated but had never done so during intercourse. Her typical pattern was to become somewhat aroused during sex play but never be able to reach a higher level. She wanted to be able to reach orgasm during intercourse.
>
> The couple reported a satisfying marriage up until one year ago. At that time, John had changed jobs to work in a company that was very interested in expansion. John felt

pressure from work on a daily basis. He always came home in an angry mood. Laurie felt that John always took out his frustrations on her; this made it very difficult for her to feel close to him when he initiated sex. At first, she participated anyway, even though she never got anything out of it. Then, she began to tell John that she was too tired, even though she really felt very angry at him. After four nights in a row without sex, John threatened to leave the relationship or have an affair unless she was more cooperative. Laurie had never lived on her own and the thought of being by herself scared her. She decided that she would try to get more involved with sex to hold the relationship together. However, she still felt herself tightening up whenever he initiated. Although she tried to deal with her uncomfortable feelings by fantasizing about a former lover during sex, she could not totally block out her angry feelings. She felt used and taken for granted. John became quite frustrated at Laurie for her passive approach to sex. For instance, she was less than enthusiastic when she performed oral sex on him; this made it difficult for him to become aroused enough to ejaculate. Eventually, he stopped initiating sex. He began spending less time at home and he criticized the way she handled the children. They often went to bed feeling very angry at each other. Laurie finally insisted that they see a sex therapist because she found the situation intolerable.

The treatment of this couple consisted of a multiple focus on different aspects of the relationship. In the initial sessions, the therapist focused on the effects of John's job change on the relationship. John recognized that his job made him very tense, but he also valued it because it was very challenging. Laurie said that she didn't know how to cope with John's frustrated and tense manner after work; he was very short with her and sometimes he didn't answer her questions at all. The therapist suggested that John be permitted about one hour of quiet time after work so that he could get more settled. This seemed a good solution, and John decided to use the time to start an exercise program. The therapist also dealt with each partner's feeling emotionally estranged from the other. For homework, the couple was told to get a baby-sitter for their two children at least twice the next week and spend some time going out to dinner and taking a walk. The couple was instructed not to have intercourse until therapy progressed to the point that both felt more comfortable. The therapist also showed the couple how to communicate what each expected from the other. They were very motivated to learn these exercises because each partner felt that the other never made requests known.

In the third session, the focus shifted to the sexual relationship. As the couple began to explore some of the problems they had, it became very apparent that John felt that sex was his domain. He had always thought that the man decided how often and when sex would occur. In fact, he had never thought much about the importance of meeting a woman's sexual needs. The therapist suggested that there was a greater probability of a more positive sexual interaction if the sexual needs of both partners were considered. Treatment then focused on the communication of sexual initiations and refusals, as well as on each partner's giving the other feedback about what types of sexual activity were most desirable. For homework, the couple was encouraged to discover more positive ways of stimulation. At first, John eagerly looked forward to these exercises simply because it meant that he would be able to get satisfaction for himself. However, he soon became interested in pleasing Laurie as well, especially when he realized that if he touched her the way that she liked, she began to respond in a very positive manner. Eventually, after a series of homework assignments that began with nongenital and moved to genital touching, intercourse was attempted. By giving John feedback about the type of thrusting that she enjoyed, Laurie was able to reach orgasm during intercourse the first time they tried, with John simultaneously stimulating her clitoris. Both were very encouraged by this progress. They felt more satisfied with sex and with the overall relationship. They were much better able to resolve the arguments that they had had in the past, and they were much more affectionate with each other.

Various other approaches have been used for the treatment of orgasm problems. Some therapists use the systematic desensitization method for women who report excessive anxiety in specific sexual situations.[10] Some women are given an assertive training approach to help them be more direct in getting their sexual needs met. Some therapists believe that strengthening the vaginal muscles may increase the woman's potential for orgasm; these therapists instruct the woman to practice contracting and relaxing her vaginal muscles.[11] For women with normal muscle tone, these exercises have not been shown to increase orgasmic capacity.[12] It is still possible, nevertheless, that women who enter therapy with poor vaginal muscle tone can benefit from vaginal exercises.

VAGINISMUS

Robin, a 20-year-old college student, had grown up believing that premarital sex was wrong. She had dated many times in high school but never had gone beyond kissing and light petting. Last year, however, she went with a date to a party celebrating the end of the semester. Her date got really high and persuaded her to go to his room. There, regardless of her protests, he forced her to have intercourse. This was a very difficult experience for Robin since she had lost her virginity. She felt that her parents would not understand if she told them about this experience; nor did she feel comfortable enough to share it with any other friends. She decided never to put herself in a situation like that again unless she really trusted the man. One year after that traumatic experience, she met a fellow student named Dave. She found him easy to talk to and she liked him immediately. They began studying together and occasionally meeting for lunch. They also began to date at night. Robin liked Dave because of his honesty and because it was very easy for her to share her feelings with him. She enjoyed kissing him and the occasional light petting they engaged in. After four months of dating, Dave told Robin that he was sexually attracted to her and that he wanted to make love to her. Robin really trusted Dave and knew that she was sexually attracted to him. But she really didn't want to have intercourse. Nevertheless, she was afraid that he would not continue to see her unless she did. Finally, after putting him off for a month, she agreed. Dave rented a motel room for the special occasion. After some wine and extended kissing, they got undressed. Although everything seemed right, Robin was so tense when Dave attempted intercourse that he could not penetrate.

When vaginal penetration is difficult, or impossible, this problem is known as vaginismus. It occurs when the outer third of the vaginal muscles contract in response to real, imagined, or anticipated attempts at penetration. The muscle contractions are not painful; in fact, many women are not even aware of them when they occur.

As in the case of Robin, vaginismus may be so severe that penetrating the vagina is totally impossible. Sometimes, only a small finger can be inserted in the vagina. For some women, it is difficult or even painful for the man to insert his penis, although the couple may be able to have intercourse after the woman becomes more aroused. In other women, vaginismus occurs only in some intercourse positions. It also may occur only with some partners and not with others. Some women with vaginismus have had many experiences of intercourse, while others have never had any. Some women with vaginismus have a strong aversion to sexual activity of any kind, while others have this reaction only toward intercourse; some of these women thoroughly enjoy sexual activity with a partner just as long as intercourse is not included. Some women with vaginismus can reach orgasm during masturbation, manual stimulation by a partner, and oral sex.

The physical factors that may contribute to vaginismus include endometriosis, injuries in the pelvic muscles, an inflexible hymen, pelvic inflammation, disease, or tumors.[13] Most cases, however, seem to be maintained by anxiety, which the woman actually may not experience subjectively. The woman's anxiety can stem from a number of sources, such as a lack of knowledge and an unfamiliarity with her own sexual anatomy. The woman may feel especially anxious about having intercourse. She may find it difficult to believe that a penis could fit in her vagina. She may fear that intercourse would result in her "being torn up inside." Some of these women have been told by parents, peers, and teachers that intercourse would be painful, especially when the hymen was "broken" for the first time.[14]

Some women with vaginismus report numerous instances of having experienced painful intercourse because of some physical problem. However, even after the problem is alleviated, the woman still anticipates pain whenever intercourse is attempted. Some women with vaginismus have a history of having been a victim of rape or incest; these experiences may make it very difficult for the woman to relax enough to allow penetration. Relationship problems can contribute to vaginismus. A woman who is in a relationship characterized by hostility may be unable to become aroused. If her partner considers sex to be a high priority, she may express her hostility toward him indirectly by experiencing vaginismus.

Treatment

The treatment of vaginismus incorporates some of the methods used to treat orgasm problems. These include educating a woman about her sexual anatomy and physiology, discovering her sexual attitudes, and obtaining information about her previous sexual interactions. Has she always had difficulty in intercourse? What have her sexual interactions been like? What is she thinking about before and during sex play? What is she thinking about when intercourse is attempted? How is she feeling at those times? How has her partner typically reacted? Does he blame himself? Does she blame herself? What do they say to each other about the failure to have intercourse?

Once this and other information is obtained, the therapist may instruct the woman in various exercises designed to help her practice contracting and relaxing her vaginal muscles. A perinometer, an instrument that measures the strength of the vaginal muscles, may be used to help her increase her awareness of these muscles, and to help her relax them during intercourse.

Some women experience a very specific anxiety reaction to sex play in general, and to penetration in particular. For these women, the method of systematic desensitization, as described in Chapter 2, sometimes is used. Glass or rubber dilators also have been used to lessen the muscle tension associated with vaginismus; these range from the size of a little finger to that of an erect penis. Once in a relaxed state, the woman is instructed to insert the smallest dilator until she is comfortable with it. At subsequent times, she gradually inserts dilators of increasingly larger sizes. Then, she may be instructed to leave the dilator inside of her vagina overnight so that she can become more accustomed to having something inside of her. When she can insert a dilator the size of an erect penis without experiencing pain, discomfort, or a high level of anxiety, she is encouraged to have intercourse.[15]

Some women with vaginismus who already feel anxious about sex may become even more anxious when using dilators. In these cases, the woman may be asked to insert a finger in the vagina. Subsequently, one finger of her partner can be used.[16]

The treatment of a woman with vaginismus may also include her partner, especially if the problem seems to be an outgrowth of an unsatisfying relationship. The treatment approach is very similar to that for orgasm problems, in that the therapist attempts to alter existing maladaptive communication styles and also addresses issues such as the woman not feeling secure enough in the relationship. Treatment may be focused on establishing a commitment in the relationship and also fostering increased caring behavior. In some cases, the therapist may encourage the woman's partner to modify sexual techniques so that the woman can become more relaxed. She may be shown how to facilitate her own arousal by masturbation, or she may be encouraged to tell a partner the ways in which she would like to be stimulated. For homework, the couple may be given an assignment only to concentrate on first nongenital and then genital stimulation but not to engage in intercourse. During consecutive foreplay sessions, the man might gradually place his penis closer and closer to the vagina without attempting to penetrate. Then, he could insert one finger and then a second, and then simulate stroking motions in order to approximate intercourse. Eventually, the woman is asked to try to insert the man's penis when she is more relaxed.

In some cases, the treatment of vaginismus includes a specific focus on reducing the woman's anxiety. This is shown in the case below.

Linda, a 24-year-old college student, was referred by her gynecologist when she complained of an inability to have intercourse. The gynecologist reported that there were no physical reasons for the problem and that the pelvic examinations had been very difficult in the past. Her vaginal muscles clamped down so tightly that neither a speculum nor a finger could be inserted in her vagina.

Linda felt that she was avoiding relationships with males because of her sexual problem. She had been involved in a steady relationship with one man for about five years, during which time they unsuccessfully attempted intercourse. Both, however, enjoyed oral sex. Linda was consistently orgasmic during these activities. But whenever her boyfriend attempted to penetrate her vagina she became fearful, tense, and anxious. She had had only one sexual experience since breaking up with her boyfriend a year before she entered treatment. This was a planned interaction with a male friend for the purpose of "helping me get over my problem." Their attempt to have intercourse was unsuccessful and left Linda feeling even more frustrated.

Linda reported that sex was a taboo subject of discussion in her home. She began masturbating when she was nine years old, which made her feel guilty and ashamed. She expected that actual penetration would be excruciatingly painful. When asked to relax, close her eyes, and imagine sexual scenes that the therapist was describing, she enjoyed the scenes until the therapist said that her partner's penis was entering her vagina. Then her eyes shot open and she exclaimed, "I can't! I can't imagine that!"

One aspect of treatment involved asking Linda to explore her genitals by touching and looking at them in a mirror. At the same time, she was asked to focus on her feelings about her body. For additional homework, she was instructed to practice contracting and relaxing her vaginal muscles daily while focusing on her sensations in the vaginal area. The therapist also spent a number of sessions discussing her past relationships with men and her anxiety about sex (excerpts from this case are presented in Chapter 2).

After six sessions, Linda was able to insert one of her fingers into her vagina. She was thrilled to discover what everything felt like and she was surprised that she experienced no pain or discomfort. She gradually inserted larger and larger dilators into her vagina. After much difficulty, she finally inserted a dilator that approximated the size of an erect penis. At this point, she was confident that she would be able to have intercourse. Overall, she felt more self-confident, comfortable with her sexuality, and interested in having intercourse when the situation was right for her. She was not in a relationship when she terminated therapy. However, a follow-up telephone call three months later revealed that she had established a satisfying sexual and emotional relationship with a man. After some initial difficulty, they were enjoying intercourse without any recurrence of vaginismus.

PAINFUL INTERCOURSE

Teresa and her husband, Joe, a couple in their 30s, had been married 12 years. They both considered themselves to have a good relationship in general. Yet both were dissatisfied with their sex life. Teresa enjoyed hugging Joe and she liked kissing him. However, it was always difficult for her to relax when he initiated sex. She always tensed up, and though she tried to think of sexual thoughts and told herself to relax, she just did not feel comfortable whenever Joe began touching around her genitals. During intercourse, she would experience mild to moderate pain in the male-on-top position, although she did not experience pain in the rear-entry position. But this contributed to an unsatisfactory sexual repertoire. Characteristically, Joe would kiss Teresa for a short while, stroke her breasts, turn her around, and then penetrate. After a while, the rear-entry position also became somewhat painful to Teresa if Joe thrusted vigorously. Thus, she began to avoid sex since she almost always experienced more discomfort than pleasure.

When a woman experiences painful intercourse (the technical name for this is dyspareunia), she may experience the pain at the opening of the vagina or deep in the vaginal barrel.[17] She may experience pain only during penetration, or the pain may continue throughout intercourse. The pain may become worse when the man penetrates more deeply, or, as in the case of Teresa, it may be experienced in some sexual positions and not in others. Also, a woman may experience painful intercourse with one partner but not with another.

Painful intercourse, like vaginismus, is considered less common than orgasm problems. In fact, painful intercourse sometimes occurs with vaginismus. The pain experienced during intercourse may be due to a milder case of vaginismus in which the vaginal muscles are tightened but intercourse is still possible. In other cases, pain is experienced without any reflexive contractions of the vaginal muscles.

The physical factors that may contribute to discomfort or pain during intercourse include vaginal infections, insufficient vaginal lubrication, a structural abnormality of the pelvis, a thick hymen, endometriosis, cysts, tumors, or scarring from pelvic surgery.[18] The psychological factors are similar to those associated with vaginismus. A high level of anxiety experienced in sexual situations often is reported. Some women have had a traumatic sexual experience in the past, such as a rape, which was both emotionally and physically painful. Others grew up expecting intercourse to be painful. Sometimes, the woman's partner is not aware of her need for extended foreplay before intercourse is attempted; penetration may be painful if the woman is not aroused and if the vagina is not well lubricated. As with orgasm problems and vaginismus, various relationship problems may contribute to dyspareunia.[19]

Treatment

The treatment of painful intercourse is very similar to the treatment of orgasm problems and vaginismus, with the possible exception of using dilators. Therapists begin treatment by asking the woman questions about when she experiences painful intercourse. What is she thinking about before, during, and after sex? What is she feeling at those times? To what extent does she anticipate the pain? Are some sexual positions less painful? How much time typically does the woman spend in foreplay? What happens during foreplay? Does she reach orgasm? From which means? What are her partner's reactions to her experiencing pain during intercourse?

For women whose painful intercourse seems to be maintained by sexual anxiety in specific situations, the therapist may use the systematic desensitization procedure described in Chapter 2. If the woman has a partner, the therapist may encourage the couple to communicate their preferences for sexual stimulation. Sometimes, the therapist assigns sensate focus exercises for homework so that the couple can practice nongenital and genital touching to facilitate sexual arousal. In some cases, the woman may not experience painful intercourse if it is attempted when the woman is sufficiently aroused; in these cases, the therapist helps the woman to be more assertive about when she is and is not interested in sex and to attempt intercourse only when she is ready.

In some cases, a more extended treatment focus on the couple's relationship is needed. This is shown in the case below.

Barry, aged 25, and Maureen, aged 21, had been married for two years. They had not had intercourse for the last two months because Maureen always experienced pain. Before that time, Barry would initiate sex by kissing Maureen for about a minute, stroke her breasts for a short while, place his finger inside her vagina, and then, at the first sign of lubrication, attempt to penetrate. She almost always experienced considerable pain at this time, which intensified when he increased his thrusting motion prior to ejaculating. Maureen had repeatedly told Barry that she needed more time before intercourse but he never seemed to understand what she meant. Barry began to feel that he was not a good lover, and that he was not sexually desirable. In addition to the sex problem, the couple had other difficulties. For a long time, Maureen had been very angry at Barry because he did not seem to accept her parents or her friends. Barry came from a higher social class than she did. As such, he considered his friends to be more sophisticated and "better people" than her parents or the friends she had before they got married. He also had some very set ideas about the way he wanted to live his life. This ranged from making decisions about where to go on vacations to what kind of movies to see. In essence, Barry ran the relationship.

In the initial session, the therapist recognized that both partners actually contributed to Barry's dominance of the relationship. Maureen had never felt secure or safe enough to express her needs in a direct manner. Her silence, therefore, gave Barry the message that she wanted him to take control over her life. Maureen agreed that it was often very difficult for her to express her needs directly because she grew up with the notion that the man was always the boss. Yet she felt that she was just as important as Barry and that she wanted more of a voice in making decisions. She also said that she was tired of placing her friends and family in the background. She said that Barry knew all about her family and friends when he married her and that there was no reason for the couple to socialize only with his friends.

After both partners were given the opportunity to discuss their feelings about these issues, the therapist underscored the need for give and take in the relationship. The therapist suggested that Maureen's painful intercourse likely was at least partially due to Barry's lack of awareness of how to arouse her. It also was suggested that her angry feelings played a part in inhibiting her arousal. For homework, the therapist first gave an assignment that asked each partner to take equal responsibility for deciding which social activities to engage in and whom to socialize with. Barry and Maureen worked out a compromise in which they would alternate spending time first with one set of friends and then with the other. If Maureen or Barry wanted to spend time away from the relationship with their own friends and family, that was considered acceptable. The therapist also stressed the importance of both partners getting their needs met during sex. The therapist gave an assignment for the couple to engage in nongenital touching for 20 minutes, with a 10-minute focus on each partner; subsequently, genital touching was added.

After 11 sessions, Barry had become much more tolerant of Maureen's family and friends, and he discovered that he actually enjoyed some of the social contact with them. The couple's sexual interactions became much more meaningful for both, and Maureen reported feeling much more sexually aroused than she had previously. She no longer was experiencing any pain. From observation of the couple in the last session, it was apparent that Maureen was much more open about her feelings and no longer took a passive stand.

In recent years, sex therapists have become much more aware that many men and women have sexual desire and arousal problems. Some even avoid sex altogether. As we discuss in the next chapter, these problems often surface only in the context of a relationship.

REFERENCES

1. W. M. Sotile, P. R. Kilmann, A. Scovern, "Definition and Classifications of Psychogenic Female Sexual Dysfunctions," *Journal of Sex Education and Therapy* 3 (1977), pp. 21-27.
2. Shere Hite, *The Hite Report* (New York: Dell, 1976).
3. L. G. Barbach, *For Yourself: The Fulfillment of Female Sexuality* (New York: Doubleday, 1975).
4. L. G. Barbach, *For Each Other: Sharing Sexual Intimacy* (New York: Doubleday, 1982).
5. J. LoPiccolo, W. C. Lobitz, "The Role of Masturbation in the Treatment of Orgasmic Dysfunction," *Archives of Sexual Behavior* 3 (1972), pp. 163-171.
6. L. G. Barbach, "Group Treatment of Preorgasmic Women," *Journal of Sex and Marital Therapy* 2 (1974), pp. 139-145.
7. J. B. Kuriansky, L. Sharpe, P. O'Connor, "The Treatment of Anorgasmia: Long-Term Effectiveness of a Short-Term Behavioral Group Therapy," *Journal of Sex and Marital Therapy* 8 (1982), pp. 29-43.
8. B. Zilbergeld, C. Ellison, "Desire Discrepancies and Arousal Problems in Sex Therapy," in *Principles and Practices of Sex Therapy*, ed. S. R. Leiblum and L. A. Pervin (New York: Guilford Press, 1980).
9. W. H. Masters, V. E. Johnson, *Human Sexual Response* (Boston: Little, Brown, 1966).
10. W. M. Sotile, P. R. Kilmann, "The Effects of Group Systematic Desensitization on Orgasmic Dysfunction," *Archives of Sexual Behavior* 7 (1978), pp. 477-491.
11. A. H. Kegel, "Sexual Functions and the Pubbococcygeus Muscle," *Western Journal of Surgery* 60 (1952), pp. 521-524.

12. P. A. Roughan, L. Kunst, "Do Pelvic Floor Exercises Really Improve Orgasmic Potential?" *Journal of Sex and Marital Therapy* 7 (1981), pp. 223–229.
13. H. S. Kaplan, *The New Sex Therapy* (New York: Brunner/Mazel, 1974).
14. S. R. Leiblum, L. A. Pervin, C. H. Campbell, "The Treatment of Vaginismus: Success and Failure," in *Principles and Practice of Sex Therapy*, ed. S. R. Leiblum and L. A. Pervin (New York: Guilford Press, 1980).
15. W. Sotile, P. R. Kilmann, "Treatment of Psychogenic Female Sexual Dysfunctions," *Psychological Bulletin* 84 (1977), pp. 619–633.
16. Kaplan, 1974.
17. W. H. Masters, V. E. Johnson, *Human Sexual Inadequacy* (Boston: Little, Brown, 1970).
18. A. R. Abarbanel, "Diagnosis and Treatment of Coital Discomfort," in *Handbook of Sex Therapy*, ed. J. LoPiccolo and L. LoPiccolo (New York: Plenum, 1978), pp. 241–260.
19. A. A. Lazarus, "Psychological Treatment of Dyspareunia," in *Principles and Practice of Sex Therapy*, ed. S. R. Leiblum and L. A. Pervin (New York: Guilford Press, 1980).

Chapter Five

SEXUAL DESIRE, AROUSAL, AND PHOBIA PROBLEMS

People differ in how often they want sex. Some desire sex every day, or more than once per day, while others do not seem to care if they have sex infrequently, or not at all. Similarly, people differ in their ability to become aroused; some can get sexually aroused fairly easily while others experience little, if any, subjective arousal even if some physiological signs of arousal (i.e., erection for the man, vaginal lubrication for the woman) are apparent. Still other people fear sexual contact to the extent that they avoid sex play altogether. In this chapter, we discuss sexual desire, arousal, and phobia problems. These sometimes contribute to or coexist with the sex problems discussed in the last two chapters.

SEXUAL DESIRE PROBLEMS

Lou and Irene, a couple in their early 40s, had been married for 15 years and had three children. Until the last year, they had a mutually satisfactory sex life. On the average, they had sex about three times each week. Lou had a job as a salesman for a liquor-distributing company, while Irene worked at home raising the children. She had always wanted a college degree but had decided to postpone it because she wanted a family. Finally, when her youngest child was old enough to be in school, she discussed returning to school with Lou. He was somewhat resistant to the idea since he thought that it would be hard for her to continue raising the children. Nevertheless, he consented and she enrolled in three classes. It soon became apparent that Irene's commitment to her schoolwork while attempting to take care of the home was an overload. She began to ask Lou to help her with household responsibilities such as going shopping for food, getting supper ready, taking care of the children when she had to study for exams, and driving them to school in the morning and to their afterschool activities. Lou began to take on more and more of the responsibilities that he considered to be Irene's. When she was home, she was either hurrying to eat so that she could study or she was too tired to interact with him. Gradually, he began to resent her for not being attentive to his needs for companionship. At times, he felt so angry at having to change his life-style and at being neglected that he did not follow through on household tasks that he had agreed to do; he sometimes "forgot" to buy groceries and he often did not clean the house. These angry feelings interfered with his desire for sex. Whereas before he had initiated fairly frequently, his initiations gradually decreased. He also began to refuse Irene's initiations, which became more frequent. When she wanted to know why he was no longer interested in sex, he told her that he was too tired from helping her around the house. Eventually, he told her that he was thinking of leaving the marriage because he was not getting his needs met.

Sexual desire is defined in terms of how frequently a person wishes to have sex.[1] Some therapists, such as Helen Kaplan,[2] make the assumption that a desire problem only exists when a person expresses little or no desire for sex. This way of thinking is difficult for us to accept since it implies that "more sex is better." Furthermore, we do not have an absolute way to determine when a person's level of sexual desire is "too high" or "too low." Consider a man who desires sex three times a week. If his partner is interested in sex once a month, is his desire too high? Or is his partner's desire too low? What if his partner instead desires sex ten times a week compared to his three times a week? In her estimation, he may have a low sexual desire.

We believe that it is not justifiable to apply one arbitrary standard of sexual desire for everyone. Thus, terms used to describe a person's sexual desire as "too high," "too low," or "inhibited" are not appropriate. Instead, we agree with sex therapists Bernie Zilbergeld and Carol Ellison that a person's sexual desire is best defined in comparison to a partner's. In some couples, one partner has a higher level of desire and the other a lower level; this is known as a "sexual desire discrepancy."[3]

Many couples in which each partner prefers a different frequency of sex reach a reasonable, or at least tolerable, compromise in some way. For other couples, however, reconciling different levels of sexual desire between partners is not a simple task. A typical pattern is that the partner with the higher level initiates sex more frequently than is desired by the other partner. As a consequence, the lower partner begins to perceive the higher partner as highly demanding and interested only in personal gratification. The partner with a lower desire may refrain from any displays of physical affection, such as a kiss or a hug, because of the fear that the higher partner will interpret these as indicating an interest in sexual activities. Over time, the partner with the higher desire may feel rejected or deprived, especially if it appears that the lower partner is taking on a passive and uninterested role during sex and submitting to sexual advances only out of a feeling of obligation. Each partner subsequently begins to feel unappreciated and unloved. This seems to be the most frequent pattern when it is the woman who has the lower sexual desire. When the man's desire is lower, he tends to avoid sexual contact altogether; the uninterested man may be worried that he will not get an erection, whereas an uninterested female can have intercourse without really getting aroused.

Why do some people have lower sexual desire? In general, people learn unique ways of responding to the different cues in the world. Some people are unable or unwilling to acknowledge the cues or stimuli that might be considered sexual by others.[4] Yet a variety of more specific factors can influence lower sexual desire. Often, the person experiences anxiety about having sex. This may stem from a restrictive upbringing, performance demands, or fears of intimacy.[5] A person may have been raised in a home in which sex was not discussed, nor considered an activity that could be pleasurable. The person may not expect to become aroused from sex so it is engaged in only infrequently. This often makes it difficult for the person to feel anything but anxiety in sexual situations, which, in turn, results in sex having a relatively low priority. Other persons experience anxiety whenever a partner complains about the low frequency of sex in the relationship and/or that sex is generally unsatisfying; after an initial attempt to please the partner by having more sex and by "trying" to enjoy it, the person typically becomes even less interested.

Some individuals with lower sexual desire are very high-strung and tense, and have a great deal of difficulty relaxing in general. Often, they experience anxiety in response to nonsexual, outside pressures, such as from a job or whenever they become overwhelmed with family responsibilities. Because they consistently are anxious, it is difficult for them to identify sexual feelings. Yet for some, interestingly enough, a high level of anxiety does not necessarily have a negative influence on sexual performance; a man's anxiety might not interfere with his ability to gain an erection, nor might a woman's anxiety inhibit her ability to reach orgasm fairly consistently. Other individuals with lower sexual desire do not experience a great deal of generalized anxiety but characteristically are moody and depressed. As a general rule, they refrain from participating in any potentially pleasurable activities, including sex. It is as if they do not want to or don't feel able to put their depressed feelings aside to obtain any satisfaction from any aspect of living.

Lower sexual desire sometimes is attributed to a person's difficulty in labeling sexual feelings and "giving in" to them. This often means that it is difficult for the person to respond to a sexual initiation; thoughts may turn to unfinished job responsibilities, what the kids are doing, a bridge game, plans to go shopping the next day, the unattractive attributes of a partner, or anything other than sex. If the person feels obligated to respond instead of simply and politely refusing a partner's sexual initiations, the person eventually becomes less and less interested in having sex. Additionally, it becomes even more difficult for the person to switch from nonsexual thoughts and feelings to sexual ones whenever a partner initiates. The person who has a problem in making this necessary transition often experiences lower sexual desire, especially if a partner repeatedly chooses a time and place to have sex that is not conducive to the person being in a relaxed frame of mind.

Many individuals with lower sexual desire have a nonsexual self-image; they do not consider themselves to be sexual beings or sexually attractive. They cannot imagine that anyone would be interested in having sex with them. Many have sex merely to please a partner or to have children, but not to obtain any pleasure from the experience for themselves. Some always have separated sex and love; they find it difficult to be in an emotionally committed relationship that includes frequent sexual contact. Still others find it difficult to get emotionally close to a partner. They may have had numerous unsuccessful relationships in the past and they do not wish to get close to a partner again; having sex infrequently helps them to maintain emotional distance. Some grew up with idealized, unrealistic expectations from sex. A woman may have expected that her first sexual experience would be an earth-shattering event characterized by multiple orgasms and feelings of ecstasy. When this does not happen, she may consider herself to be sexually inadequate.

What about individuals with a higher level of sexual desire? Typically, they become very easily aroused from thinking about sex and from observing sexual scenes on television or at the movies. Some are very interested in pornographic materials. Some respond to almost every sexual opportunity available. They initiate sex very frequently. They are easily bored with a routine sexual sequence. As such, they often attempt to make sex more exciting by persuading a partner to experiment; this may include wanting to have sex in a variety of different ways and places.

Some people with higher sexual desire define a wide variety of cues as sexual. They may interpret feelings of happiness, tenderness, frustration, anger, physical exhilaration, *and* anxiety as indications of sexual excitement. A woman that Peter Benchley describes in the novel *The Deep*[6] fits this style of interpreting cues: "To Gail, sex was a vehicle for expressing everything—delight, anger, hunger, love, frustration, annoyance, even outrage. As an alcoholic can find any excuse for a drink, so Gail could make anything, from the first fallen leaf of autumn to the anniversary of Richard Nixon's resignation, a reason for making love" (p. 63).

Many persons with a higher sexual desire characteristically have used sex as a way to feel better about themselves. If a partner agrees to have sex, the person feels important. Often, these feelings are enhanced if it is evident that the partner really enjoys the experience. But if a partner refuses sex, the person may feel hurt, undesirable, and unworthy. This is highlighted below.

Andy met Marie in college. After dating for one year, they got married. Marie soon discovered that Andy wanted sex very frequently. He often initiated sex three times a day, and sometimes in the middle of the night as well. Marie began to question Andy's high interest in sex. She began to wonder whether this was all that he wanted from marriage. She told him that she felt like an object rather than like a person. This only made Andy initiate more frequently. He became angry that Marie was not as interested in sex as he was. Her constant refusals not only made him feel very inadequate as a lover but suggested to him that she was not committed to the relationship. Marie did many things that showed her devotion to Andy. She would bring him lunch at the office even though it meant that she gave up time to play bridge with her friends. She often typed for him at times that were very inconvenient for her. At home, she waited on him "hand and foot." Marie became very frustrated and angry at Andy because of his constant focus on sex, his unwillingness to believe that she still could be committed to him and yet not be as interested as he was in having sex so frequently, and his lack of understanding of her needs. She became so exasperated that she told him she didn't care if he had sex with other women just as long as she didn't find out about it.

Treatment

Most often, a sexual desire problem surfaces in the context of a relationship. However, some clients without a partner seek treatment because they wish to increase their level of sexual desire; usually, prior partners have complained that sex occurred too infrequently in the relationship. For these clients, the therapist first attempts to discover why the client has had difficulty. Some have associated sexual desire with being a bad person, or as a sign of promiscuity. For these clients, Jerry Friedman[7] and other sex therapists focus on the irrational beliefs that may be inhibiting sexual desire. The client might be asked to substitute rational for irrational statements. For example, when the client begins to experience guilt about sexual desire, making rational statements to oneself, such as "I am not a bad person because I desire sex" or "I am in control of my sexual behavior," can help one accept sexual desire as a healthy rather than as a pathological indicator.

Clients who wish to increase their sexual desire often are unable or unwilling to acknowledge the cues that might be considered sexual by others. For these clients, the therapist may assign a book of sexual fantasies or encourage the client to see a pornographic movie. Suggestions also might be made for widening the range of situations and feelings that evoke the sexual desire. The client may be encouraged to try using sex (rather than watching television or reading) as a relaxing and pleasurable activity after a hard day at work. The client is asked to imagine what it would be like to have an enjoyable sexual interaction and to focus on the specific details that may be considered most pleasurable. For example, a woman who might be attracted to her partner's chest or buttocks would be asked to imagine stroking and feeling that area. A man who finds oral sex pleasurable might be asked to imagine that he and his partner are having oral sex.

Some clients with lower sexual desire always have felt uncomfortable about sex. Accordingly, the therapist focuses on the factors that contribute to these feelings. For clients who feel awkward about their ability to provide sexual pleasure, the therapist suggests various sexual techniques. For clients who harbor angry feelings toward the opposite sex in general, the therapist encourages the client to deal with these feelings; this process may involve a role-play interaction, with the client expressing angry feelings toward a past partner while imagining that the partner is in the same room.

According to sex therapists Jerry and Laurel Oziel,[8] a sexual desire discrepancy is one of the most, if not the most, difficult of sex problems to treat. This is because treatment usually involves a greater coordination of each partner's unique ways of viewing sex, and also an extended focus on the factors in the couple's interaction that contribute to the desire discrepancy. In treating a couple, some sex therapists focus on raising the sexual desire of a partner who desires sex less often; typically, the goal of treatment is to increase the frequency of sex in the relationship to meet the expectations of the partner with the higher desire. We do not agree with this focus for the reasons mentioned at the beginning of this chapter. Instead, it makes sense to us that treatment should focus on the expectations and behaviors of both partners.

As a first step in approaching a desire discrepancy problem, the therapist assesses the nature of the discrepancy, and the couple's unique attempts to deal with it. How often does each partner want sex each week? Who typically initiates? What is the typical sequence of sexual activities? How has the partner with the lower desire coped with the other partner's greater desire? Does one partner avoid sex by going to bed early or by being a non-participant during sex? How else have the partners attempted to cope with the discrepancy? Are they angry at each other? What needs are being met by the discrepancy and which are not?

The partner with the lower sexual desire might be asked to specify his or her optimum conditions for sex. What time of the day or night is the person most interested? What would this person's ideal sexual interaction consist of? Which specific sexual activities in which sequence? For instance, chest stimulation followed by oral sex or the other way around? What are some ways that the other partner can foster increased sexual desire? By taking a shower or bath right before sex? By verbally expressing positive statements about the partner's desirability? By holding and cuddling without these behaviors being followed by intercourse? By making reassuring statements of the person's desirability at various times throughout the day rather than just before or during sex?

What about the partner with the higher sexual desire? The therapist asks similar questions about this partner's sexual experiences and reactions to sex. Has this partner always desired sex more frequently in prior relationships? Is sex engaged in for pleasure, or does sex meet other needs as well, such as to reduce tension, to gain reassurance, or to dominate one's partner? What does it mean to the person when one's partner is not interested in sex? Is it a devastating blow to the person's self-image? Does the person feel unloved, or can a refusal be accepted without the person becoming upset?

The therapist also asks questions to determine whether any relationship problems are maintaining the desire discrepancy. Is each partner able to communicate with the other? How are decisions made? Which responsibilities are shared and which are not? What is the level of love and attraction in the relationship? How is affection communicated, if at all? Are both partners excited to be with each other, and if not, why not?

In some cases, the therapist merely suggests to the couple various ways to improve the quality of sex. This can include spending more time in foreplay, each partner paying attention to the other's sexual preferences, sex occurring only at a mutually acceptable time and without outside distractions. For some couples these modifications are all that is necessary for the partner with lower desire to want sex more frequently. In other couples, the partner with the higher desire becomes satisfied with a reduced frequency of sex because it is much more pleasing when it occurs.

For still other couples, however, the solution to a desire discrepancy is not so simple. The partner with higher desire may insist that a high frequency of sex is a priority in the relationship, while the other partner just doesn't consider sex to be that important. The therapist may not be able to resolve the discrepancy using the above-mentioned suggestions. Instead, other strategies are used. Let us assume that the partner with a higher sexual desire primarily uses sex to enhance self-worth; the therapist may encourage this partner to use nonsexual ways of getting these needs met from the relationship. Sometimes, this is possible if the lower partner kisses and hugs the partner with the higher desire more often, or by praising the partner for positive, desirable attributes, such as physical attractiveness or the way that he or she is dressed. The therapist also encourages the higher partner to do the same for the lower partner.

Some couples with a desire discrepancy get into difficulty when the partner with the higher desire level consistently initiates and the lower partner consistently gives in. For these couples, the therapist may ask the partner with the higher desire to consider at the point of initiation whether sex is really what he or she wants or whether some other type of emotional or physical contact, such as a verbal expression of affection or a hug, can satisfy that need just as well. The partner with the lower sexual desire is told to respond to a sexual initiation only when really in the mood. Typically, the partner who feels able to refuse an initiation without the other partner becoming angry feels more in control of sex. This can make such a partner more receptive to sex at other times. Instead of giving in, the partner can decide whether some nonsexual activity such as cuddling or taking a walk could be shared as an alternative, or whether even some time away from the partner is preferred. Once both partners feel equally in control over when sex occurs, the quality of sex often improves and sometimes the frequency also increases. When one partner is not interested, the couple may be encouraged to set an appointment for sex at some future time. A verbal expression of affection, such as "I really do care about you a great deal, but how about sex tomorrow morning?" may be sufficient.

Some desire discrepancies are attributed to each partner's wanting to have sex for different reasons. One partner may consider sex to be "good medicine"; sex makes the person feel better when in a bad mood. In contrast, the other partner may not want any physical contact at all when feeling down. It is easy to see that a conflict is likely if both partners are moody and the first partner initiates sex to feel better. For these couples, the therapist helps each partner to understand what the other wants from sex, as well as to verbalize to each other about the desire for sex *before* sex is initiated.

The therapist may give a homework assignment so that both partners can practice meeting each other's needs. One way that this is done is to ask each partner to submit a list to the other, one day in advance, of the kinds of nonsexual activities that he or she would find pleasurable. Both partners then look over the list and either agree or disagree to meet the requests. Then, one partner makes a commitment to engage in the agreeable behaviors on the list the next day. The day after that, the other partner does the same. From this exercise, each partner is provided the opportunity to give as well as to receive pleasure from the other; this is assumed to generalize to the sexual interaction.

In cases in which the desire discrepancy seems to be maintained by each partner not feeling comfortable to express feelings such as anger, hurt, happiness, or sadness to the other, the therapist asks the couple to express these feelings during role-play interactions in the office. The couple then is given an assignment to verbalize these feelings to each other at home whenever they are experienced. After partners feel comfortable in communicating nonsexual feelings, a greater likelihood exists that sexual feelings also can be communicated. Sometimes, George Bach's fair-fight training methods[9] are used to help couples resolve power struggles and conflicts that are maintaining the desire discrepancy. When partners are no longer angry at each other, the partner with the higher desire may be less interested in a high frequency of sex, especially if this partner uses sex for reassurance about being loved. The lower partner, in contrast, may be more interested in sex than previously because the angry, unsettled feelings are replaced with sexual ones.

For homework, the therapist may assign various exercises to enhance the sexual relationship. A couple may be encouraged to share their sexual fantasies, to read erotic books, and look at erotic movies together. The therapist may suggest that the couple add specific techniques to the sexual repertoire, such as oral sex or different intercourse positions. The therapist may suggest that the couple take turns in developing a sexual scenario with their preferred setting and sequence of sexual activities. Each partner may be asked to write down a favored scenario and then, if the partner agrees, it is acted out. One such scenario might involve the man pretending that he is a telephone repairman working in the woman's home and then she attempts to seduce him or vice versa. An advantage of these scenarios is that they give each partner a chance to develop a preferred sexual script that is found to be most arousing. In addition, the therapist also may give nonsexual homework assignments that are designed to facilitate sexual desire. For some couples, merely taking a walk, listening to music, or spending some quiet time at the end of each day by lying next to each other and discussing daily events can help put both partners in a sexual mood. But even if sex does not occur, both often feel closer after sharing time together. This is illustrated in the case below.

> Peggy, a 32-year-old lawyer, and her husband, Brian, a 35-year-old executive, came in for therapy with the complaint that their sex life was not what it used to be. They both agreed that they had had "great sex" during the first five years of their marriage but that things had gotten progressively worse since the birth of their son last year. They used to have sex about five or six times a week, but the frequency had decreased to once every week or two. Brian preferred to have sex at least once every two days. Peggy said that she just wasn't interested in sex anymore and that when they did have intercourse, she did not enjoy it. Their usual sexual interaction consisted of a short period of foreplay and intercourse for about two minutes.
>
> It was evident that Peggy and Brian were attempting to maintain high-pressure careers while sharing the responsibilities of caring for their child. Peggy was somewhat resentful because she felt that Brian was not taking on his fair share. Brian, in contrast, felt that he was doing far more than most husbands and that Peggy ought to appreciate the amount of time that he did spend with the baby. They were no longer taking the time to be alone together that they had in the earlier years of their marriage. Peggy was under a lot of stress in her job and felt that she was not receiving adequate emotional support from Brian.

The therapist decided that the desire discrepancy and sexual dissatisfaction could be addressed only after each partner viewed the overall relationship more positively. Peggy and Brian were instructed to take at least one hour of each day to spend alone together, talking or sharing some activity. In addition, they were to go out on a "date" together once each week. The therapist helped them work out a more equal and mutually satisfying division of child-rearing responsibilities. Some initial resistance was encountered because it seemed that Brian still held to the notion that child-rearing is basically the woman's job. After confronting these beliefs and discussing their agreement for equal responsibility prior to deciding to have a child, Peggy and Brian were able to find a workable solution for themselves. They decided to make more use of nearby family members who offered to care for the child in the evenings occasionally.

As the couple became more relaxed with each other, parenting seemed to become less of a chore and more of an enjoyable, shared activity. They would joke about whose turn it was to get up in the middle of the night to attend to their crying child, and sometimes they would both decide to get up and do it together. By this time, sex had become more leisurely. They began to spend their assigned time alone together taking long baths with each other, snuggling up in front of the fireplace with a bottle of wine, and sharing other intimate activities, which eventually led to more relaxed and enjoyable sexual interactions.

SEXUAL AROUSAL PROBLEMS

Liz and Gene, a couple in their late 30s, had been married for two years. Liz had two children from a previous marriage, while Gene had never been married before. He always had been highly interested in his career as a lawyer; he worked long hours and he had built up a successful law practice. As was his custom when he was single, he often brought his work home with him. After a while, Liz realized that she and Gene always talked about his work whenever they were together. On the weekends, he was too tired to socialize with their friends or go out dancing, which she had always enjoyed. Numerous times, Liz attempted to talk to Gene about what went on in her life during the day and some of the problems that the children were having. But after a few nods of his head, he would change the conversation and begin talking about himself and his cases. Liz became more and more angry about not feeling important in the relationship, and about Gene not spending enough time with the children. Her ruminations about her angry feelings made it difficult for her to become aroused during sex. Gene began to feel inadequate as a lover since Liz no longer was as responsive to his touching as she had been. He began to lessen his efforts to arouse her and became concerned only with his own satisfaction; usually, he ejaculated within 30 seconds after penetration.

Sexual arousal refers to how "turned on" or how sexually excited the person feels. We consider it to be a subjective state rather than a physiological response. One person may feel highly aroused sexually and yet not show physical signs of sexual excitement, such as an erection or vaginal lubrication. Another person may not *feel* turned on even though he or she experiences these physiological signs of excitement.[10]

Often, low sexual arousal and low sexual desire are experienced together. There may be a discrepancy, however, between an individual's level of sexual desire and level of sexual arousal. A person may want to have sex quite frequently but be unable to become aroused. Less commonly, an individual may not be interested in sex but may become aroused anyway.

Many therapists believe that low sexual arousal is a prime cause or maintainer of sexual difficulties such as erection problems, ejaculatory inhibition, and orgasm problems. In fact, therapists often attempt to increase the client's sexual arousal in treating these problems.

The factors influencing a person's ability to become sexually aroused are considered to be similar to those influencing sexual desire. An individual with low sexual arousal may feel anxious about sex and guard against experiencing any sexual feelings. Many have learned to associate pleasurable feelings with negative emotions.[11] Some are just too tired when a sexual opportunity presents itself. They may have used up all of their energy on the job, in taking care of the kids, or on their hobbies. Sex has never held much of a priority. Some have learned to repress their sexual feelings while growing up and have channeled their interests into nonsexual matters. Others do not seem to become aroused about anything. They go through life feeling fairly apathetic about most events and sex is no exception. Feelings of depression are common, to the extent that life often is not enjoyed.

Treatment

As noted earlier, sex therapy with clients who have orgasm problems, erection problems, and ejaculatory inhibition involves various methods to increase sexual arousal. Thus, the treatment of a sexual arousal problem involves asking many of the same questions that are asked for the treatment of these sex problems. Some clients with low sexual arousal, however, are able to function successfully when they have sex.

Through homework, the client with low sexual arousal is taught to become more comfortable with sexual feelings. The client may be encouraged to look for sexual cues in a variety of ways, such as when watching television commercials, reading magazine advertisements, and seeing a movie. The client may be asked to buy a partner a stimulating bottle of cologne to use, or to suggest that a partner wear clothes that might be arousing. Also, the therapist may suggest that each partner act as if he or she were extremely aroused during sex by exaggerating moans or sighs of ecstasy; this often makes it easier for the client to feel more comfortable in "letting go" during sex. This exercise also gives both partners practice in giving and receiving feedback in response to sexual stimulation. From sensate focus exercises, the client can practice focusing on the sexual stimulation without being distracted with thoughts about whether the partner is enjoying the experience.

The therapist also may attempt to facilitate the client's sexual arousal by suggesting that the client focus on a favorite sexual fantasy at various times throughout each day, as well as just before sex occurs. Clients who have difficulty in conjuring up a particular sexual fantasy may be assigned to choose one from reading a book of sexual fantasies, such as Nancy Friday's *My Secret Garden*.[12] This type of assignment is useful for clients who have difficulty in concentrating on sexual stimulation because of interfering thoughts about work, shopping, or the kids; the client is instructed to counteract these interfering thoughts by closing the eyes and becoming absorbed in a favorite sexual fantasy while receiving sexual stimulation. Clients also are told to have sex only at a mutually agreeable time and place so that they can begin to concentrate on sexual stimuli sometime before then.

Some clients with lower sexual arousal do not feel in control during sex; their feelings of powerlessness inhibit their ability to become aroused. For these clients, the therapist may help them construct a sexual script so that the clients can feel more in control of the sexual situation. Each partner takes on a role designed to maximize the client's perceived optimal conditions for reaching a high level of sexual arousal. Included in the script could be instructions on how to undress a partner, what words to say during the experience, and the type of stimulation that is desired. One such script could include one partner pretending to be asleep on the bed while the other attempts to arouse the partner in provocative ways. Eventually, after the client experiences higher levels of sexual arousal, the therapist suggests that the client focus on the specific stimulation that is being received. The client is asked to look at the partner's hands while being stroked and to experience the sensations that are evoked. In addition, clients are asked to become absorbed in the most arousing aspect of a partner's body, whether it be the partner's facial features, chest area, genital region, buttocks, or legs. In this manner, the client gains practice in maximizing arousal by shutting out outside distractions and, instead, becoming totally involved in the experience.

Individuals differ in the extent to which engaging in a specific sexual behavior contributes to their level of sexual arousal. For instance, one partner may prefer engaging in oral sex prior to intercourse since this sequence always has enhanced his or her sexual arousal. But the other partner may not like oral sex. The therapist working with such a couple may explore the reasons for this "sexual behavior discrepancy." The woman always may have thought that oral sex is disgusting. Once her attitudes are discussed openly, she may want to reconsider. The therapist then may help her to discover the specific ways that her partner would like her to conduct it; she may even get more aroused herself from noting her partner's pleasure as she engages in oral sex. In some cases, of course, one or both partners may not wish to experiment; it usually follows that certain sexual behaviors then are considered "out of bounds."

Partners not only differ in the sexual behaviors that they prefer to facilitate their sexual arousal but they also differ in the time they prefer to spend in these behaviors. A woman who usually becomes aroused very easily may want to engage in oral sex soon after sex play begins; in contrast, her partner may want to spend a considerable amount of time in kissing and stroking before oral sex. For such a couple, the therapist might attempt to slightly increase the arousal of the man by making suggestions that he have sex only when he is really interested, that he focus on the most stimulating aspects of his partner's body as soon as sex play begins, and that he "hold back" his attempts to arouse his partner until he "catches up" to her level of arousal. The therapist might tell the woman to focus on pleasing the man during the early stages of sex play until he feels sufficiently aroused to have oral sex. This type of compromise, of course, would be difficult to resolve if one partner wants to have intercourse almost immediately after sex play begins, while the other wants to wait. Other "sexual sequence discrepancies" that are somewhat difficult to resolve include one partner wanting intercourse whenever sex play is engaged in but with the other partner also occasionally preferring mutual genital touching or mutual oral sex without subsequently having intercourse. One solution for this discrepancy might be both partners making their requests for sex known to the other before sex play begins so that one or both partners are not disappointed if their "favorite" way of having sex does not occur. Both partners then can focus on the intended sexual agenda without expecting possible disappointment.

Sometimes, clients with low sexual arousal are shown how to use the excitement they experience in nonsexual ways to generate sexual excitement. Therapists Bernie Zilbergeld and Carol Ellison treated a woman who experienced little sexual feeling but got a "high" from playing tennis. She was taught to associate the feelings of exhilaration, emotional arousal, and physical excitement she experienced while playing tennis with sex. Among other assignments, she was instructed to swing her tennis racquet around in the bedroom prior to sex to help increase her level of sexual arousal. Eventually, she reported a greater responsiveness to sexual situations.[13]

SEXUAL PHOBIA PROBLEMS

Diane, a 29-year-old elementary school teacher, had never been comfortable with any kind of sexual contact. These feelings appeared to stem from having been sexually molested by her stepfather on a fairly regular basis during her adolescence. Although she had discussed her angry and confused feelings about these experiences with a therapist five years ago, she still had a basic distrust of men. Hence, she dated only infrequently. Whenever her dates would attempt to have sex, she strongly rebuffed them. She had told herself that she wanted only friendship relationships with men because she was afraid of being used for sex. She had never really gotten sexually aroused when thinking about sex; in fact, she rarely thought about it at all.

Then, at a Christmas party, Diane met Rick, a very humorous, sensitive 33-year-old accountant. Both immediately discovered that they had a lot in common. They liked attending cultural and sports events. Diane, however, told Rick of her interest in keeping the relationship only as a friendship. Rick did not consider this an obstacle; he told her that he was not interested in an intimate relationship but he just wanted a companion to do things with occasionally.

After getting together on a regular basis for two months, Rick expressed his desire to get closer to Diane, and his desire for sex to be a part of that closeness. Diane was flattered. She told him that even though she thoroughly enjoyed his company and found him to be quite attractive, she was not interested in sex. She told him that she had never felt comfortable with sex, and she did not want to lead him on to think that she would be interested in the future.

One night, after attending a show, Rick and Diane went to a nightclub. They danced often and they had more than a few drinks. When Rick took Diane home, he decided that "it was now or never." He attempted to kiss and fondle her and was immediately rebuffed. He told Diane that he wanted to go to bed with her and that he could no longer see her unless she wanted this also. Even though Diane didn't want to stop seeing Rick, she felt so anxious about the possibility of having sex that she decided to end the relationship.

Individuals with a sexual phobia problem experience intense feelings of anxiety and panic in sexual situations.[14] Some, like Diane, become anxious in response to any physical contact, such as holding hands or an affectionate hug, or even when sex is discussed or viewed in a movie. Others are afraid only of actual physical contact and can be comfortable with erotic materials or discussions about sex. Some enjoy most aspects of sex but have a strong anxiety reaction to a specific sexual activity, such as oral sex.

Few sexually phobic individuals express much interest in sex. Lower sexual desire and sexual phobias, however, are different problems. An individual with low sexual desire is not interested in frequent sexual activity, but there is not an active avoidance and fear of sex as is typical of sexually phobic individuals. Sexually phobic individuals who tolerate sex, despite their anxieties, are likely to have difficulties in becoming sexually aroused or reaching orgasm; thus, many have other sexual problems. Some individuals who have a sex problem such as those discussed in Chapters 3 and 4 avoid sexual contact because of a fear of failure. These individuals do not have an actual sexual phobia. A man with an erection problem avoids initiating any sexual contact because of the embarrassment and frustration he experiences when he cannot get an erection. He may want to have sex, but he avoids it because he does not want to fail.

A sexual phobia may severely limit an individual's relationships. A person without a partner may avoid dating because of the fear of sex. Otherwise positive relationships may end if an individual panics when any kind of physical contact is attempted, or when the individual refuses sexual initiations. The partner of a sexually phobic individual may feel frustrated, rejected, inadequate, or resentful. The sexual phobia thus may contribute to conflicts in the overall relationship as well.

The factors that contribute to sexual phobias are not well known. Some individuals have associated sex with fear and pain. They may have had a traumatic sexual experience in the past, such as a rape or incest. A woman's former husband may have always used physical force during sex; as a consequence, she is uncomfortable whenever her dates make sexual advances. Other sexually phobic individuals have been severely reprimanded for various forms of sexual expression as they grew up. During his adolescence, a man's parents may have ridiculed and punished him when he was discovered masturbating. A woman may have been severely punished by her parents when they discovered her having sex with her boyfriend in the basement of her home. If the individual subsequently experienced similar negative reactions concerning sexual behavior, any sexual activity may now evoke anxiety and guilt. Of course, some sexually phobic persons are anxious in general and more prone to panic in a variety of situations, not just sexual ones.

Treatment

Initially, the therapist attempts to discover the factors that contribute to the sexual phobia. Is the client's reaction tied to numerous negative sexual experiences under certain conditions but not others? Does the reaction manifest itself with a particular partner or with all partners? What does the person think about and feel when sex is discussed? When a partner initiates sex? How much does the client feel in control of the sexual interaction? What does the person imagine to be the ideal conditions for desiring sex? What is the ideal initiation? What is the ideal sexual interaction? Which activities are included?

Once this information is obtained, the therapist attempts to reduce the client's avoidance of sex. Some sexually phobic individuals also have other sexual problems, such as a difficulty gaining an erection or a difficulty reaching orgasm. When this is the case, the sexual phobia is treated first since the client probably will not show any improvement in sexual functioning until the intense anxiety that has become associated with sex is diminished.

Typically, it is too anxiety-producing for many sexually phobic clients even to participate in nongenital caressing until greater comfort is experienced in less involved interactions. For homework, therefore, the therapist first may assign sexual exercises that aim only to help the client feel comfortable with very minimal physical contact. In very small steps, the client progresses slowly to more and more physically intimate interactions. A couple may begin with merely talking about sex while holding hands. Then, the partners might be asked to lie side by side fully clothed before any nude body contact is attempted. If too much sexual activity is attempted at any point in treatment, the sexually phobic client may experience an overwhelming level of anxiety and avoid a commitment to attempting the homework.[15] Thus, it is necessary for the client's partner to be highly cooperative and very patient throughout the treatment process. Eventually, the couple may attempt intercourse if the exercises previously engaged in are accomplished with only a minimal level of anxiety and discomfort, and if the client feels ready to do so.

In some cases, the therapist may suggest that the client use medication to help reduce the anxiety experienced in sexual situations. The method of systematic desensitization (see Chapter 2) is used most often when the sexual phobia is specific to a particular aspect of sex, such as in response to vaginal penetration.[16] Sometimes it is used in a case of a generalized anxiety reaction to sex, such as in the case below.

Janet, a 30-year-old newly divorced woman, felt very anxious whenever confronted with a possible sexual situation. She had gotten married when she was 18 years old. Before her marriage, she had had very few dates. Her husband was a very controlling person who usually made all the decisions for both of them. He was very protective of her; he frequently called her at home while he was at work to make sure that she was safe. He did not feel comfortable with her going out at night unless he or someone he trusted was with her. She was very dependent on him and really didn't feel as though she had a life of her own. The marriage ended when he came home one day and told her that he was in love with somebody else.

It took Janet over a year to get over the shock of being left for another woman. Although many men were interested in dating her, she rarely dated. Whenever one of her dates made a pass at her, she told him that she was just not ready to have sex.

Six months before she sought treatment, Janet was raped by a security guard while working late at her job as a secretary. It was very difficult for her to get over the initial shock of the rape experience. She frequently had nightmares and "flashbacks" of the situation. She also became very frightened of men; whenever a man began to talk to her, she became very tense and anxious. She coped with these feelings for a while by avoiding situations where she might be in a vulnerable position. She never went out at night by herself. Even though her friends occasionally had wanted to introduce her to various men, she had not accepted a date since the rape incident. She felt very scared at the thought of being alone with a man.

In the first few sessions, the therapist explored Janet's reactions to her marriage. She acknowledged that she had depended on her husband much too much for security and that she needed to "grow up." She had never really talked about herself to anyone else. Consequently, she was very eager to discuss what her childhood was like. Like her former husband, her father had always been the head of the house. She rarely was given any responsibility for taking care of herself, but she always felt protected by her family. She admitted that she married her husband because he had characteristics very similar to her father's. In the fourth session, the therapist encouraged Janet to talk about her rape experience. She had never really discussed the details of the experience with anyone else before, and she became quite upset when she described what happened and her reactions to the event. She knew that the rape had made her withdraw from men. She felt only a small degree of anxiety when kissing a man, but she became very tense if any further physical contact was attempted. She was most anxious at the thought of being vulnerable in a sexual situation.

The therapist used the systematic desensitization method to treat Janet's sexual anxiety. A hierarchy was formed that included items focused on her anxiety in social and sexual situations. As each item on the hierarchy was "passed," Janet attempted the same item in real life. For example, if she was able to imagine herself going to lunch with a man without experiencing any undue anxiety, she was then given an assignment to accept an invitation from the next interesting man who asked her. The therapist also focused on helping Janet to feel more in control of her interactions with men. Doing role-playing exercises, the therapist helped her to practice making requests for what she wanted from her dates, and from sex. These requests included the following: "I would like to go to the movies with you but then I have to go home and get some sleep" and "I would like to kiss and hug you but I'm not ready for any further physical contact at this point."

In the next few months, Janet had numerous positive dating experiences. She also was fortunate enough to begin dating a man, somewhat older than herself, with whom she really felt comfortable. After they had had five dates and he didn't make any sexual advances, Janet told him that she was receiving treatment for her anxiety about sex, and she appreciated the fact that he had not pushed her. He told her that he liked her a lot and he had thought that she might be uncomfortable about sex. Janet trusted him to the extent that she asked him if he would be willing to help her by participating in some of her sexual home-work assignments. The man was very patient and, even though he never attended the sessions, he agreed to approach the relationship at her pace. By attempting the step-by-step sexual exercises mentioned above, Janet eventually was able to have intercourse with him while experiencing only a minimal level of anxiety. These feelings decreased in subsequent interactions to the point that she eventually reached orgasm. In her 14th and last session, Janet was very enthusiastic about her treatment gains. She said that she was much more comfortable in her ability to state her needs in a straightforward manner, and she was very satisfied with her current relationship.

As sex therapy has grown in popularity, more therapists have attempted to use the methods to treat the sexual problems of diverse populations. These are discussed in the next chapter.

REFERENCES

1. B. Zilbergeld, C. Ellison, "Desire Discrepancies and Arousal Problems in Sex Therapy," in *Principles and Practices of Sex Therapy*, ed. S. R. Leiblum and L. A. Pervin (New York: Guilford Press, 1980).
2. H. S. Kaplan, "Hypoactive Sexual Desire," *Journal of Sex and Marital Therapy* 3 (1977), pp. 3–9.
3. Zilbergeld, Ellison, 1980.
4. Ibid.
5. L. LoPiccolo, "Low Sexual Desire," in *Principles and Practice of Sex Therapy*, ed. S. R. Leiblum and L. A. Pervin (New York: Guilford Press, 1980).
6. P. Benchley, *The Deep* (New York: Bantam, 1977).
7. J. M. Friedman, "A Treatment Program for Low Sexual Desire" (Paper presented at Society for Sex Research meeting, Charleston, S.C., June 1982).
8. Jerry Oziel, Ph.D., Laurel Oziel, M.S.W., Beverly Hills, California, personal communication, December 1982.
9. G. Bach, Y. Bernhard, *Aggression Lab—The Fair-Fight Training Manual* (Dubuque, Iowa: Kendall/Hunt, 1971).
10. Zilbergeld, Ellison, 1980.
11. H. S. Kaplan, *Disorders of Sexual Desire* (New York: Brunner/Mazel, 1979).
12. N. Friday, *My Secret Garden* (New York: Pocket Books, 1973).
13. Zilbergeld, Ellison, 1980.
14. H. S. Kaplan, A. J. Fyer, A. Novick, "The Treatment of Sexual Phobias: The Combined Use of Anti-Panic Medication and Sex Therapy," *Journal of Sex and Marital Therapy* 8 (1982), pp. 3–28.
15. Ibid.
16. A. Lazarus, "Overcoming Sexual Inadequacy," in *Handbook of Sex Therapy*, ed. J. LoPiccolo and L. LoPiccolo (New York: Plenum Press, 1978).

Chapter Six

SEX THERAPY WITH OTHER POPULATIONS

Sex therapy has treated a wide variety of individuals and couples, most of whom probably have been young to middle-aged, able-bodied, in reasonable physical health, and with a heterosexual orientation. To a lesser extent, sex therapy methods also have been used with other populations, often requiring a somewhat different focus and a consideration of different issues.

It is beyond the scope of this book to discuss the treatment of sexual problems of all of the different people who have received sex therapy. In this chapter, we briefly discuss sex with seven populations: the elderly, persons with a homosexual orientation, persons with lifelong physical disabilities, persons with spinal cord injury, and persons with coronary or kidney disease or cancer.

SEX THERAPY WITH THE ELDERLY

Over the years, a popular misconception held by the American public is that the elderly do not have sexual needs and desires. When an older person is known to be sexually active, others often respond with disapproval, humor, or disbelief. Statements such as "He's just a dirty old man" or "You shouldn't be doing that at your age" are more typical than not. Consider the following anecdote.

A 62-year-old woman married a 70-year-old man who was recently widowed. It was her first marriage, and although family members were shocked and disapproving, she felt that the marriage would provide needed companionship for her old age. Having had limited sexual experiences in her life and believing the traditional notions of diminished sexual interest in old age, she held no expectations for sexual satisfaction in the marriage. Shortly after the marriage she decided to confide in her 20-year-old niece about her husband's sexual advances. In a bewildered and embarrassed state, she asked, "What do you do when he wants it every night?" The rather surprised niece could think of no other response but "Turn over and go to sleep."

While the physiological changes associated with aging certainly affect sexual activity, the changes and the time of onset vary from person to person. What are these changes?

As he ages, a man usually finds that it will take him more time to gain a full erection. He may no longer be able to do so spontaneously merely from kissing and touching. A reduction in seminal fluid occurs so that the force of the ejaculation lessens. The penis returns to a relaxed state more quickly after ejaculation, and it takes considerably longer for a subsequent erection. In the later years, if he loses his erection during sex, he may not be able to gain another one for 12 to 24 hours even if he has not ejaculated.[1] Of course, an apparent advantage of the aging process in men is that the reduced urgency for ejaculation often leads to greater ejaculatory control. As a consequence, the man often is able to have intercourse for a longer period of time than when he was younger.

Elderly men often report that their ejaculations are more diffuse, sensual experiences, in contrast to the intense, genitally focused ejaculations of their youth. Typically, they report a reduced need for ejaculation and diminished sexual interest. A man in his 60s and 70s often is satisfied with one ejaculation or less per week.[2]

The physiological changes in women are less dramatic

than in men. Vaginal lubrication may be slower and/or lessened. The walls of the vagina may become thinner so that they are more easily irritated. Although women retain the capacity for multiple orgasms throughout old age, their orgasms usually are less intense. Following menopause, however, the woman's desire for sex may be heightened. In fact, some women just begin to recognize their full capacity for sexual expression in their middle and older years. Many feel less inhibited about acknowledging their sexual feelings. The elimination of the fear of pregnancy and the necessity for using contraceptives is helpful in this regard.

The contrast in the physiological and psychological changes that occur in males and females may create adjustment difficulties. Many men consider their ability to have sex an important aspect of their masculinity. When they notice a decline in their functioning, considerable anxiety and panic may result. They may avoid sex altogether. Women whose partners manifest a decreased interest in sex often feel guilty if they desire sex more frequently than their partners.

Often, real (and sometimes imagined) physical problems interfere with sexual functioning in old age. Older people reflect a higher incidence of cancer, heart disease and related difficulties, diabetes, and arthritis. Many elderly men have vascular, neurologic, and hormonal problems that may contribute to erection problems. Some elderly persons do not want to have sex because of the possible pain associated with physical problems. Or a partner may refrain from sex because of the possible risk of harm. Medications, which often must be taken on a regular basis, also may interfere with sexual responsiveness.

Sex therapy with the elderly often includes a focus on helping the client to understand the physiological and corresponding psychological changes associated with the aging process. Couples may be asked to increase the time spent in foreplay activities, and advised not to consider intercourse and orgasm to be the ultimate goals. They may be asked to relearn flirtation techniques and give each other more verbal and physical affirmation of their sexual desirability.[3] The following case is typical of sex therapy with an elderly couple.

> Frank and Evelyn, age 78 and 75, had been married 47 years when they responded to an advertisement for a sexual treatment program. Their primary complaint was a marked decrease in sexual activity, which they both acknowledged but had been reluctant to discuss with each other. They had a mutually satisfying marriage and both had enjoyed an active sex life. In the initial session, Frank reported that he had had occasional erection problems in the last few years. As his problem occurred more frequently, he began to avoid sexual initiations, feeling that he was "over the hill." Evelyn had interpreted his less-frequent initiations and his erection problems as evidence of her declining attractiveness. She felt that she did not "turn him on" anymore since he had always taken the initiative and been highly responsive in the past.

The therapist discussed the effects of aging on sex. Frank was encouraged to verbalize his attraction to Evelyn more often. The couple was asked to engage in sensate focus (see Chapter 2) to eliminate Frank's concern about needing to reach an erection for sex play. Evelyn was encouraged to initiate sex and to take a more active role in stimulating Frank's genitals, with his guidance and feedback. She was instructed to guide Frank in manually stimulating her, according to what she had learned from masturbation. They became more willing to experiment and to expand their repertoire of sexual behaviors. They discovered that they both enjoyed cuddling and touching without intercourse. Frank found that he could gain a sense of satisfaction from helping Evelyn to reach orgasm without worrying about reaching an erection and ejaculation himself. He began to gain and maintain erections more regularly as Evelyn took a more active role in sex.

SEX THERAPY WITH HOMOSEXUALS

Practically the same sexual problems experienced by heterosexuals seem to occur in persons with a homosexual orientation. The one exception seems to be that lesbians rarely seek therapy for vaginismus or painful intercourse since these difficulties, by definition, relate to sexual intercourse; yet the same responses may occur if vaginal penetration is attempted with a finger or an artificial penis. Orgasm problems are the most frequent among lesbians seeking sex therapy. Ejaculatory inhibition, which is considered the least common sex problem in heterosexual men, seems to be more common than premature ejaculation in homosexual men.[4]

The same sex therapy methods are used to treat homosexuals as are used to treat heterosexuals. An example is the case of Dave, a 41-year-old lawyer who did not have a regular partner.

Dave sought treatment because of an erection problem. He was able to maintain an erection during kissing and foreplay, but his penis became flaccid whenever he attempted anal intercourse. His sexual history included a marriage that lasted eight years as well as numerous "one-night stands" with homosexual lovers. Dave reported heightened anxiety feelings whenever he was in a potential sexual situation.

Using the systematic desensitization procedure, the therapist asked Dave to imagine various sexual scenes, which began with Dave and his partner going to a gay bar and having a few drinks. The scenes then shifted to the ride to Dave's house. Then, Dave was told to imagine initiating kissing and touching with a man whom he was attracted to. The final scenes on the hierarchy focused on Dave's anxiety over possibly losing his erection if he attempted penetration. After five sessions, Dave successfully engaged in anal intercourse.

In addition to treating the sex problem, sex therapy with homosexuals often includes a focus on conflicts that may be caused by factors unique to gay relationships. Typically, gay relationships are kept hidden from family and friends due to anticipated disapproval. A couple may feel a need to pass as "just roommates." Maintaining secrecy can be stressful on both partners. Thus, treatment may include dealing with the stress associated with being homosexual in a heterosexual world, and its effects on the sexual relationship.

Sex therapists also have begun to better understand the sexual needs of people with various physical disabilities. Any serious condition that affects a person's body— such as an illness, injury, or surgery—often limits or changes in some way the ability to have sex. Below we discuss the influence of various physical disabilities and medical conditions on sexual functioning and the ways in which sex therapy has been used with these populations.

LIFELONG PHYSICAL DISABILITIES

Individuals with disabilities such as cerebral palsy and severe curvature of the spine have never been "able-bodied." Often, they have been brought up under various restrictions. Because of mobility problems, many are more closely supervised by parents and other authority figures. They live in what therapist Robert Chubon[5] refers to as a "more censored world." They often miss out on developing social skills and experimenting with sex. Parents of disabled children tend to be overly protective to spare them the pain of social and sexual rejection. Overall, the disabled have less opportunity to establish sexual relationships because of limited mobility and, often, institutional restrictions. Due to negative societal stigmas, they are less likely to be viewed as sexually desirable mates.

Many persons with lifelong disabilities have undergone frequent and sometimes humiliating medical and surgical treatment throughout their childhood. Some report experiencing a mind–body split, feeling dissociated from their own body, in order to cope with the constant intrusions. Victoria Thornton,[6] disabled with cerebral palsy since birth, describes the following experiences.

> And then there were the clinical examinations. I can remember going for diagnostic tests when I was three or four years old, as well as the weekly physical therapy, and no one ever asked me, "How do you feel about my touching you?" I didn't have the connection between my mind and body that all people need to express themselves sexually. . . .
>
> I would get out there in my underwear in front of the doctor, the physical therapist, a couple of teachers, maybe the principal, other kids and parents. I'd be paraded around and had to listen to my "case" being discussed. . . . When I did get out of my braces and stood alone without them for the first time, in some ways it was a reward, but it scared me to death in other ways. I had no way to relate to my body anymore.

Sex therapy may include exercises to foster more positive feelings about the body. The therapist also may help clients deal with the realistic possibility of social rejection because of their disability, and to develop social skills to help them feel more comfortable with others.

SPINAL CORD INJURY

Individuals with a spinal cord injury experience paralysis and a loss of physical sensation in response to touch or temperature. The level of the injury determines how much of the body becomes paralyzed. Many .men retain their ability to obtain reflex erections but most cannot ejaculate.[7] Women often experience natural vaginal lubrication and normal physiological changes when aroused. Physical sensation in the genital region often is lost in both men and women, and the ability to experience a "normal" orgasm usually is lost. However, persons report orgasm experiences characterized by intense physical sensations and/or emotional closeness.[8] In some cases, a person's emotional reactions to the injury, such as depression and grief, may precipitate a decrease in sexual desire. Even a long period of time after the injury, the person may evaluate himself or herself as unattractive and sexually undesirable. Family, friends, and health care providers often reinforce the misconception that the person now is an asexual human being.

Don Smith,[9] a sexuality and disability educator who suffered a spinal cord injury at age 19, recounts some of his feelings and experiences.

> Then I broke my back body surfing in 1968. What this did for me was to confirm all the feelings I had that I wasn't worthy of love. I was sure I wasn't worthy of love now. I was sure I was somebody who couldn't give love now. I was sure that I was somebody whom no one would be interested in. . . .
>
> When I think back to when I broke my back—that tremendous hurt and anger and emotion that you feel at the time—I swallowed it all because I was a "man." When I think about it now, it makes me angry that my feelings were bottled up like that. I spent four years after my injury

being asexual, but feeling very needy, not having any way to get that good human contact. That luxurious feeling of having someone lay next to you in bed—having someone to hug, someone to go home and hold, was missing in my life. I really felt that I needed it.

Sex therapy with spinal cord-injured individuals often emphasizes improving their feelings about their body. Discussion may center around the following questions: How would you describe your body? What parts of your body do you like? What parts don't you like? Do you like the texture of different parts? For homework, clients may be instructed to sit or lie in front of a mirror naked. They are told then to visually and, if possible, tactually explore their entire body. If they have use of their arms, they can touch both paralyzed and nonparalyzed parts of their body. They are instructed to pay attention to how they feel about these parts. By exploring clients' reactions to the exercise, information can be gathered on whether they have accepted the paralyzed parts of their body and whether they can appreciate their attractive qualities. A focus on these reactions can foster more positive feelings about their worth as sexual and sensual persons.

The therapist also may challenge prevailing myths about sex for the disabled. Clients are encouraged to acknowledge their needs for affection and sexual expression, and to explore the range of their sexual response (i.e., erectile or orgasmic ability, sensitivity of various body parts). Through exploration, practice, and focusing attention on new sensations, the client is encouraged to reach a higher level of sexual awareness. The client may discover that nonparalyzed areas of the body are more sensitive to touch than previously imagined.

Clients are taught how to adapt their sexual interactions to their physical limitations using experimentation and creativity. A spinal cord injury involves specific changes in the person's mobility and flexibility. This often necessitates making changes in the manner that sex occurs, and in the behaviors that are engaged in. For some persons, intercourse or certain sexual positions commonly used in the past may no longer be physically possible. In these cases, the client may be shown how to instruct a partner in viable intercourse positions or in alternative modes of stimulation to accommodate the physical limitations. A man may sustain an injury that makes it impossible for him to support himself in the man-on-top position during intercourse. He and his partner may have to reorient their thinking to acknowledge the practicality of the woman-on-top position. Some couples may need to add new sexual behaviors to their sexual repertoire. Or they may need to emphasize sexual behaviors that they previously engaged in to a lesser extent. The establishment of a new sexual repertoire may require corresponding sexual value changes. Initially, the disabled person or a partner may have negative reactions to sexual alternatives such as masturbation or oral sex.

CORONARY DISEASE

Many people survive heart attacks each year. Once the immediate fear of death has passed, the patient begins a readjustment to living with the limitations imposed by coronary disease. Only about one-quarter of the people who are sexually active prior to a heart attack resume normal sexual activity afterwards.[10]

Although restrictions are placed on a cardiac patient's physical activities, the vast majority can have intercourse safely if the energy requirements do *not* exceed their physical limitations. A nitroglycerine-type preparation taken prior to sexual intercourse usually can allow the couple to be sexually active again when anginal pain is a problem, but this may not lessen the anxiety they feel about the possibility of another heart attack. Some cardiac patients find themselves trying not to get very excited during sex so they will not strain their heart. This is understandable after such a life-threatening experience. However, it also may interfere with sexual functioning and enjoyment.

Many of the sexual problems of cardiac patients stem from emotional reactions to the disease. Depression, feelings of inadequacy, or a lowered sense of self-worth are often experienced, which may influence sexual interest and expression.

Therapy often focuses on helping a person to accept and adjust to the necessary life-style changes following a heart attack. Women who undergo coronary bypass surgery seem to be much more concerned about resuming household and job responsibilities than about resuming sexual activity.[11] In some cases, these concerns need to be addressed before a focus on sexual adjustment. Any specific sexual problems that have occurred, such as a difficulty gaining an erection, are treated with the same methods described in Chapters 3, 4, and 5.

KIDNEY DISEASE

Individuals with chronic kidney disease, formerly considered a "terminal" illness, now are able to survive for many years. However, they usually need to be connected to a dialysis machine for 12 to 24 hours each week to maintain life. Although a kidney transplant is possible, the new organ may be rejected by the body and the patient then must receive dialysis treatment.

Most renal patients, even those with successful transplants, report a decrease in sexual interest.[12,13] A large number of males also report erectile or ejaculatory problems, and females often report difficulty reaching orgasm.[14] The relative contribution of physical and psychological factors is unclear. Feelings of depression and anxiety, as well as feelings of being tired, weak, or "sickly," are commonly associated with the disease. Therapy often is directed toward alleviating these feelings and helping the client adjust to any nonsexual and sexual changes that must be made as a result of the illness.

CANCER

Surgery has saved the lives of many persons with cancer. Often, however, surgery results in the removal of body parts that can influence a person's sexual self-image. For instance, a woman who has had a mastectomy often feels mutilated, unattractive, and "only half a woman." She may fear sexual rejection and thus avoid sex. It may be difficult for her to be sexually responsive because of a preoccupation with her missing breast(s) or the belief that her partner no longer finds her sexually attractive.

Group treatment sometimes is used to help mastectomy patients better accept the loss of a breast. From sharing common feelings, women are taught ways of dealing with partners' reactions and of reestablishing a sense of wholeness and desirability as sexual beings.[15] Emotional recovery from a mastectomy is strongly influenced by the reaction of the woman's partner. Many men are unsure of how to provide support during this time and are confused about their own reaction to the loss. Body imagery exercises in the partner's presence and sensate focus exercises may be used to help both partners to accept the reality of a missing breast.[16]

Ostomy surgery, often performed for cancer of the bladder, rectum, or colon, necessitates the creation of a permanent opening in the body. Patients must wear a pouch to collect body excrements. People who have undergone ostomy surgery must adapt to a new way of eliminating bodily wastes; they may be limited in the type of clothing they can wear, and the pouch may get in the way during sexual interactions. Patients who are in a stable relationship when they undergo surgery may fear rejection from their partner or question why their partner would want to stay with them. Patients without partners face the issue of how and when to explain their disability to a new partner. Some people may avoid sex because they are concerned about others' reactions to their disability. Damage to nerves or scars from surgery may cause sexual problems, such as painful intercourse or erection difficulties.[17]

One young woman,[18] who underwent radical surgery for cancer of the vagina, relates some of her experiences and reactions to this major life change.

> I began to experience depression over the losses of my body parts, of the "healthy" young woman I once was and over the helplessness of my situation. I was overwhelmed by the nerve loss to my pelvis and was, to my surprise, totally incontinent of urine and bowel. . . .
>
> The first attempt at intercourse was a mess. My bladder leaked all the more. My innervation to my genitals was still not present. Orgasm was nowhere for me. Tears and tears could not express my feelings of this added loss. It seemed the unexpected things would never stop. I began to question why he stayed with me. What was in it for him to have a girlfriend who was mutilated and disfigured? . . .
>
> The incontinence made my life complicated by having to have extra paraphernalia: a catheter, urinary bag on the leg during the day, a larger collecting bag for the night, pads, plastic pants, plastic sheets for the bed, an extra set of

clothes in case the urine leaked through to my clothing. It
was unappealing in every way and unacceptable to my sexual image. . . . The years have brought me an acceptance of
the cancer and my surgery. The growth in my ideas and
experiments with sexuality have increased greatly since my
surgery. What was most helpful was being able to share my
experiences with people who could understand and be
accepting and finding people who were trained and had
accurate information on how I could help myself.

Therapy for persons who have had ostomy surgery
may focus on body imagery, acknowledging the client's
depression, and ways of accommodating the collection
pouch during sex. Different sexual positions may be suggested to avoid rubbing the pouch. Clients also may be
taught how to experience satisfaction during sex without
intercourse and/or orgasm as goals.

And so, many people representing different populations have received sex therapy. How effective is sex therapy anyway? In the next chapter, we present the results of
the research that has attempted to answer this question.

REFERENCES

1. H. S. Kaplan, *The New Sex Therapy* (New York: Brunner/Mazel,
   1974).
2. W. H. Masters, V. E. Johnson, *Human Sexual Response* (Boston: Little,
   Brown, 1966).
3. M. A. P. Sviland, "Helping Elderly Couples Become Sexually Liberated: Psychosocial Issues," *Counseling Psychologist* 4 (1975), pp. 67–
   72.
4. D. P. McWhirter, A. M. Mattison, "Treatment of Sexual Dysfunction
   in Homosexual Male Couples," in *Principles and Practice of Sex Therapy*, ed. S. R. Leiblum and L. A. Pervin (New York: Guilford Press,
   1980).
5. Robert Chubon, Ph.D., Assistant Professor, Rehabilitation Services
   Training Program, University of S.C., Columbia, S.C., personal communication, 7 July 1982.

6. V. A. Thornton, "Growing Up With Cerebral Palsy," in *Sexuality and Physical Disability*, ed. D. G. Bullard and S. E. Knight (St. Louis: C. V. Mosby, 1981), pp. 26–29.

7. T. M. Cole, "Sexuality and the Spinal Cord Injured," in *Human Sexuality*, ed. R. Green (Baltimore: Williams and Wilkins, 1975).

8. S. Bregman, "Sexual Adjustment of Spinal Cord Injured Women," *Sexuality and Disability* 1 (1978), pp. 85–92.

9. Don Smith, "Spinal Cord Injury," in *Sexuality and Physical Disability*, ed. D. G. Bullard and S. E. Knight (St. Louis: C. V. Mosby, 1981), pp. 12, 14.

10. R. A. Stein, "Sexual Counseling and Coronary Heart Disease," in *Principles and Practice of Sex Therapy*, ed. S. R. Leiblum and L. A. Pervin (New York: Guilford Press, 1980).

11. S. Althof, C. Coffman, "The Effects of Coronary Bypass Surgery on Women's Sexual Functioning" (Paper presented at the Society for Sex Therapy and Research meeting, Charleston, S.C., June 1982).

12. H. S. Abram, L. R. Hester, A. F. Sheridan, G. M. Epstein, "Sexual Functioning in Patients with Chronic Renal Failure," in *Handbook of Sex Therapy*, ed. J. LoPiccolo and L. LoPiccolo (New York: Plenum Press, 1978).

13. J. K. Nowinski, T. Ayers, "Sexuality and Major Medical Conditions: A Pilot Study," in *Sexuality and Physical Disability*, ed. D. G. Bullard and S. E. Knight (St. Louis: C. V. Mosby, 1981).

14. P. M. McKevitt, "Treating Sexual Dysfunction in Dialysis and Transplant Patients," *Health and Social Work* 1(3) (1976), pp. 133–157.

15. R. Kriss, "Self-Image and Sexuality after Mastectomy," in *Sexuality and Physical Disability*, ed. D. G. Bullard and S. E. Knight (St. Louis: C. V. Mosby, 1981).

16. H. H. Witkin, "Sex Therapy and Mastectomy," *Journal of Sex and Marital Therapy*, 1 (1975), pp. 290–304.

17. V. Alterescu, "Sexual Functioning Following Creation of an Abdominal Stoma," in *Sexuality and Physical Disability*, ed. D. G. Bullard and S. E. Knight (St. Louis: C. V. Mosby, 1981), pp. 46–56.

18. E. Burger, "Radical Hysterectomy and Vaginectomy for Cancer," in *Sexuality and Physical Disability: Personal Perspectives*, ed. D. G. Bullard and S. E. Knight (St. Louis: C. V. Mosby, 1981).

Chapter Seven

HOW EFFECTIVE IS SEX THERAPY?

The methods of sex therapy may be interesting and innovative, but how effective are these methods anyway? We know that clients of the other psychotherapies seem to have about an equal chance of improving, not changing, or getting worse from treatment. What about sex therapy? What kinds of changes can be expected? How long do these changes last? Which clients are likely to get better? Is sex therapy ineffective for some? What about negative or harmful effects?

In this chapter, we attempt to provide some answers to these and other questions. First, we discuss the important issue of treatment success and failure. We make some predictions about the client characteristics that are associated with these outcomes. Then we present our analysis of the results of over 140 published research studies that have investigated the effectiveness of sex therapy.

WHAT IS A TREATMENT SUCCESS?

It is very difficult to arrive at an objective definition of a treatment success. Whether the client improves and the client's satisfaction associated with the improvement seem to be the most important considerations.

Certainly, some type of improvement indicates that treatment has been helpful. But how much improvement warrants the designation "treatment success"? This is an important question because clients who improve differ in the extent of their improvement. Some experience rather dramatic gains. A woman who reached orgasm very rarely during intercourse now may do so almost every time. A man who consistently ejaculated within 30 seconds after penetration now is able to control his ejaculation consistently. A couple who complained about a desire discrepancy now is able to have sex at a mutually acceptable frequency.

Some clients do report these and other highly positive changes from sex therapy. However, most clients who improve probably are not "cured" in the sense that they never have any sexual difficulties again. A woman who rarely reached orgasm during intercourse may now do so more frequently, although not every time she wants to. Sometimes she just might not be that aroused. A man may now have greater control over his ejaculation. Nevertheless, he occasionally may ejaculate sooner than he would like, especially if his partner becomes more active than usual.

Clients who improve also differ in how satisfied they are with their improvement. Some clients are satisfied even if they improve only slightly, while others are satisfied only if they improve a great deal. Of course, much of what determines how satisfied a client feels about therapy has to do with the client's level of functioning and expectations for improvement before treatment. A woman who was never able to reach orgasm from intercourse but now does so in 40% of her attempts might be satisfied with this outcome. Another woman who was able to reach orgasm during intercourse in 60% of her attempts might be satisfied only if she reaches a 90% level after treatment.

Who decides if treatment has been successful? Should it be the therapist or the client, or should there be a mutual decision between the two? Some therapists do not seem to acknowledge the meaningfulness of relatively small gains for some clients and instead use a specific criterion of a treatment success, such as a woman's ability to reach orgasm during intercourse in 50% or more of her attempts. However, as we noted above, clients differ in the extent of satisfaction attributed to various levels of improvement. Therefore, it seems inappropriate for therapists to use one standard of treatment success for all clients. Instead, the client is the best of all possible judges. The client who is satisfied with the improvement (whether it be little or great) on some dimension (e.g., sexual functioning, communication) to the point of believing that further treatment is not necessary is a successful treatment case, regardless of the therapist's criteria.

How long should the client's improvement be expected to last after treatment ends? For a month, one year, five years, or "forever"? We really don't know. As we discuss later in this chapter, we have very limited information about the long-term effectiveness of sex therapy. We do know, mostly from clinical experience, that some clients who improve after therapy lose their gains over time. As a general rule, the longer the client remains satisfied with the improvement attributed to sex therapy, the more effective treatment has been.

WHO IS LIKELY TO SUCCEED?

Not much research has investigated the client characteristics that predict successful treatment. However, clinical observations suggest the relevance of some of these.

The client who has had a sex problem for only a short while has a much better chance of success than if the problem has existed for years. Clients of all ages have the potential to improve from sex therapy. Nevertheless, in general, clients in their 20s and 30s have a more favorable

treatment prognosis than clients in their 40s or 50s or
older; younger clients are not as likely to have had the sex
problem for as long.

Regardless of the sex problem, clients who have made
a relatively positive adjustment to life and are not suffering
from any debilitating emotional problems, such as severe
depression or anxiety, at the time of treatment are more
likely to benefit. Clients who have had numerous positive
sexual experiences before treatment have a better chance
of success than clients who have had very few, if any. Let
us consider two men who seek treatment for an erection
problem. One man reports having a successful intercourse
experience—defined as penetration leading to ejaculation—every second attempt, while another man has not
had one successful experience in many attempts over the
last five years. If both of these men have the treatment goal
of a successful intercourse experience "at least 80% of the
time," the first man certainly is closer to that goal than the
second before treatment begins. The first man is more
likely to reach that goal, and he is more likely to reach it
sooner.

Most clients want to improve in some way their ability
to have sex with a partner. Of these clients, those who are
in a good relationship are more likely to succeed. While it
is difficult to arrive at a universally acceptable definition of
a "good relationship," most of them probably are characterized by one or more of the following characteristics:
love, liking, physical attraction, mutual respect, trust, and
a sense of intimacy. Partners in a good relationship also
seem to be able to resolve conflicts in a mutually satisfying
manner. Each partner has the freedom to develop as an
individual rather than feeling stifled by the relationship.
There is a mutually acceptable balance of control and
dependency in the relationship; both partners are happy
with their roles and responsibilities. Couples who reflect

some or all of these attributes have a better foundation to work on the sex problem as a team.

Success is more likely when the client works with the therapist. This can be accomplished in several ways. The client can make every effort to give honest and complete information about past and present sexual behavior, even though it may be uncomfortable to do so. This would include volunteering any information relevant to the sex problem that the therapist might not have asked about, such as if the client is preoccupied with a past relationship, or if the client with a partner also is involved in an ongoing affair. In the latter case, therapists often recommend a separate session without the client's partner present so that the client can discuss the affair in depth without feeling restrained. The therapist who is aware of all aspects of the client's life that may relate to the sex problem is more likely to devise an effective treatment plan.

During therapy, it is important that the client ask the therapist for clarification whenever something is not understood, or if treatment does not seem sufficiently focused to meet the client's goals. The client who verbalizes real concerns and feelings as they arise has a better chance of getting the most out of therapy.

Clients also can work with the therapist by attending treatment sessions regularly and by completing homework on time.[1,2] But the client should not be so quick to accept an assignment without first considering whether it is reasonable. The therapist attempts to help the client make progress in a step-by-step fashion. Yet much of sex therapy is educated guesswork. Accordingly, the therapist is not always able to determine exactly the assignment that is just right to keep the client on track. Occasionally, an assignment may be given that really is too difficult at that particular stage in treatment. Alternatively, the therapist may not believe that the client is ready to progress to the next stage; an assignment might be given that is not sufficiently challenging. The client who gives the therapist honest feedback when treatment seems to be moving too fast or too slow enhances the likelihood of a positive outcome.[3]

WHAT IS A TREATMENT FAILURE?

Some clients do not improve at all; even after many sessions, nothing has changed. Others improve but are not really satisfied. A woman who had never reached orgasm now is able to do so from manual or oral stimulation by her partner, but she cannot do so during intercourse, which was her treatment goal. Others improve to the point of being satisfied, but then they relapse or lose their gains over time. Still other clients get worse or are harmed in some way from sex therapy. We consider all of these clients to be treatment failures, even though clients who do get worse are much more serious cases.

It is our belief that the largest category of treatment failures are clients who improve to the point that they leave treatment but subsequently lose their gains or relapse. This process can be rather sudden or it can occur gradually over a longer period of time. Two weeks after leaving therapy a man may not be able to control his ejaculation in five consecutive sexual interactions. Another man may have been able to control his ejaculation consistently for about one to two months after treatment but then he begins to realize that every now and then he does not last as long as he would like. Some of these clients return to sex therapy, while others get discouraged and try to live with the problem.

Clients who are harmed also do not get what they want from sex therapy. But they have lost much more than time or money. Treatment may have made them feel worse about themselves. The man who has had an erection problem for many years is asked to discuss his sexual history and life experiences. The more he talks, the more aware he becomes of his perpetual state of unhappiness and his adjustment difficulties. He may decide that the task of personal reconstruction is too overwhelming and he terminates treatment. Not only has he not gotten what he wanted from sex therapy (i.e., the successful treatment of the sex problem) but he feels worse because he now labels himself as a failure in life!

Couples also can experience harmful effects from sex therapy. As we discussed in Chapter 2, sex therapy with couples often focuses on much more than the sex problem. It also examines each partner's ways of interacting with the other, and the roles that each partner takes in the relationship. For couples who have relationship problems, the sessions and the homework assignments may uncover angry feelings that both partners have suppressed for a long time. Both partners may begin to feel more vulnerable than when they started sex therapy, and they may not want to continue to work on the sex problem. The couple might terminate treatment without having improved the sexual relationship, but now they no longer can deny having all these other problems. Sometimes, improved sexual functioning leads to other problems, especially if the client's partner does not attend the sessions or is not sufficiently informed about what the client has learned from sex therapy. The partner may not feel comfortable with the sexual and nonsexual changes that the client has made.[4] As an outgrowth of sex therapy, one partner eventually files for divorce. Sex therapy attempts to enhance relationships and not hurt them. Thus, a relationship breakup precipitated by sex therapy must be considered a negative effect.

WHY DO TREATMENT FAILURES OCCUR?

In sex therapy, as in the other psychotherapies, the client takes a risk. Sex therapy usually asks the client to substitute new thoughts, feelings, and behavior patterns for old ones. While the changes that are part of this process seem to be necessary for the positive effects experienced by some clients, they also can precipitate harm in others.

Our own clinical experience and our conversations with other sex therapists have suggested that treatment failures can often be attributed to one or more of the following reasons.

An Unwillingness to Carry Out Homework

Many treatment failures seem to be due to clients not taking homework assignments seriously. The client who is unwilling to do homework is not likely to improve since the sessions alone do not offer an opportunity to practice what is learned, or to give the therapist feedback about how treatment is progressing. As noted earlier, therapists sometimes give assignments that are too difficult. Yet at other times, the assignment is quite reasonable and the client is just not willing to make an effort to follow through. Somehow, job responsibilities get in the way, the kids are too noisy, or there just doesn't seem to be enough time to complete or even attempt the assignment. The case below is an example.

Bill and Marsha, a couple in their 30s, had been married for five years. Bill complained that Marsha was not very interested in sex. Marsha agreed. She felt that the problem was that she was so involved with her very demanding job as a social worker in a nursing home. After work, she was only interested in exercising, watching television for a while, and then going to sleep. Marsha said that she cared a lot about Bill and she knew that she was not meeting his sexual needs. Yet she was only interested in having sex on the weekends. Both agreed that sex was very pleasurable at those times.

After exploring the couple's sexual history, the therapist asked Marsha if she was really interested in having sex during the week. She said that she was willing to try. Her easiest workdays were Tuesdays and Thursdays, and she thought that she could get in the mood on those days. The therapist suggested that she might try thinking of an arousing sexual fantasy as she drove home. The therapist also spent some time helping both partners to communicate their sexual preferences to each other. Both agreed to an appointment for extended body caressing and feedback at 8:00 p.m. on the following Tuesday and Thursday.

Marsha was somewhat enthusiastic when she left the session and she verbalized "good intentions." Yet in the next session, it was evident that she did not really make much of an effort. She "forgot" the appointment on Tuesday and reluctantly agreed to participate in the exercise later that night. Bill was very angry at that time but he decided to go ahead anyway. He was unable to feel comfortable, however. On Thursday, just before 8:00 p.m., Marsha complained of a headache, and she didn't really want to do the exercise. Bill became very angry and told Marsha to get another job. But she was not interested in this alternative. This angered Bill to the extent that he decided further treatment would be a waste of time.

Relationship Problems

Many treatment failures occur because the client is in an unsatisfactory relationship. The client may have gotten married without really knowing that much about the partner. After the marriage, differences between partners in dealing with friends and in-laws and in their feelings and attitudes became apparent. For many years, they rarely resolve any disagreements but instead remain angry at each other. Sex is avoided by both partners going to bed at different times, or it is only engaged in as a routine event for physical release.

Many couples with these and similar problems seek sex therapy thinking that an improved sex life will salvage a very unrewarding relationship. However, the tension and hostility that has existed often is so overwhelming that it is too late. This is shown in the case below.

> Dan and Bonnie, a couple in their mid-30s, had been married for 13 years. Dan came to the first session alone. He revealed that his sex life was almost nonexistent. When he did have sex, he occasionally was not able to maintain his erection. He had had this difficulty for about one year. Dan said that he didn't know what Bonnie wanted from sex. Whenever he initiated, she would complain that he didn't know how to turn her on. She didn't like the way that he kissed or touched her. She would become very angry, berate him for not being a good lover, and then tell him that she would rather go to sleep.
>
> Dan also revealed some additional concerns. Bonnie had spent eight of the last nine years reluctantly raising their three children. Last year, Bonnie decided to enroll in four courses. These were quite difficult and she had to spend a considerable amount of time studying at home and at the library. Often, she did not come home until ten o'clock. This left Dan responsible for cooking, cleaning, and taking care of the children, all of which did not fit with his idea of the male role.

The therapist realized the importance of including Bonnie in treatment and suggested that Dan ask her to participate with him. In the next session, both partners expressed a great deal of anger toward each other. Bonnie was very angry at Dan for not being more understanding about her commitment to school and to her eventual career. She insisted that she no longer wanted to be a housewife and a caretaker of the children, and that Dan had to realize that. She said that sex was just not that important to her anymore. Usually, her schoolwork took up most of her energy, and she didn't have as much sexual interest as in the past. She also didn't like the way that Dan made sexual advances. But she expressed a willingness to improve their sex life. A few days later, however, Bonnie telephoned the therapist and said that she was not physically attracted to Dan, nor did she believe that she ever would be again. She emphatically stated that she was leaving the marriage.

Lack of a Steady or Cooperative Partner

Some goals for improved sexual functioning probably do not require the participation of the client's partner in treatment. Two examples are a woman who wants to reach orgasm from masturbation, and a man who wants to develop greater control over his ejaculation. However, some clients may be treatment failures because they do not have a partner to help them work on the sex problem. The case of Fred is an example.

Fred, a 51-year-old divorced business executive, had been unable to gain an erection sufficient for penetration in intercourse in the last two years. His eight-year marriage had been characterized by considerable tension and conflict. He began to have such difficulty in maintaining his erection that he and his wife stopped having sex altogether. Just when he had decided that sex was not important to his wife, he came home and found her in bed with another man. The marriage ended shortly thereafter.

Since his divorce, Fred spent most of his free time reading books in his apartment. Sometimes he went out with a few friends after work. The few dates that he had

were unsatisfactory, primarily because he often felt pushed
to have sex. He described these sexual experiences as "dis-
asters"; typically, he gained a partial erection during foreplay but his penis became soft just before he attempted penetration. Six months ago, he started dating again but
stopped shortly thereafter because of his fear of being an
inadequate sex partner. Yet he recognized his loneliness
and felt that his life was incomplete. He had just about
given up on finding a partner when a friend arranged a
blind date for him. They hit it off instantly. Fred sought
treatment because he did not want his erection problem to
interfere with the relationship.

In the first few sessions, the therapist discussed Fred's
marriage, his doubts about his sexual performance, and his
feelings about his new relationship. Fred was very enthusiastic about treatment; however, he came to the third session in a very depressed mood because his girl friend had
told him the night before that she was more interested in
pursuing a relationship with someone else. This was very
upsetting to Fred, but he maintained his goal of an intimate relationship with a woman. After discussing his feelings about being rejected, Fred accepted an assignment to
ask a woman in his office for a date. However, she was not
interested. In the next few weeks, he again had no success;
the women he had asked for dates were not available or
interested in him. Fred again discussed his disappointment
and said that he would keep trying. Two days later, he
phoned the therapist and said that it would be best for him
to wait until he was in a steady relationship before
returning.

An Unwillingness to Work after Treatment Ends

Sex therapists typically give homework assignments
and then check on their completion. This reminds the

client of the necessity of working on the sex problem if treatment is going to be effective. Unfortunately, clients too often terminate without realizing that a relapse is possible, or even likely, if they do not remain attentive to what they learned from sex therapy. A man may have learned not to attempt intercourse when he is angry at his wife. He decides to do so anyway and discovers that he is unable to control his ejaculation again. A couple whose sex problem was partially maintained by both partners not feeling close to one another gradually may begin to let outside distractions interfere with the intimacy they had established during therapy. They may stop taking walks together or weekend trips by themselves and instead include friends or the children. Eventually, the sex problem reappears because the old behavior patterns that had maintained the problem in the first place are engaged in once again.

It would be unfair and inaccurate always to hold clients responsible for treatment failures. Certainly, the therapist may be partially, if not totally, responsible. The therapist may not have accurately assessed the important factors that were maintaining the sex problem; thus, an insufficient treatment plan may have been formulated. The homework assignments may have been "too much, too soon" for the client. The therapist may not have stressed the importance of the client working on the sex problem, or helped the client to specify treatment goals. The therapist may not have helped the couple adjust to the changes in the relationship that stemmed from the resolution of the sex problem. The therapist may not have encouraged the client to keep working after the client reported satisfaction with an improved level of functioning. And the methods used by the therapist may not have been powerful enough to foster improvement that would be maintained over time.

How many clients are successes and how many are failures? We are not able to answer this question. It is likely that many clients who either don't improve, relapse, or believe that they have been harmed from sex therapy do not inform their therapists of these outcomes; nor do many therapists follow up their clients to see what really happened. Thus, most therapists probably do not really know which of their clients improved, relapsed, or got worse over time. Let us look at the research to get an additional picture of the effects of sex therapy.

WHAT ABOUT THE RESEARCH?

It is unfortunate that so little research is being conducted while so much sex therapy is being done. Many therapists, especially those in full-time private practice, apparently do not take the time and/or lack the necessary research sophistication to undertake a meaningful evaluation of the treatment they provide. Therefore, the many clients with sex problems who have been treated in private practice settings and mental health clinics are not well represented in the research.

How representative of the outcomes of all persons who have ever received sex therapy are the treatment outcomes of the clients in the 140 studies we analyzed? Not very. Scientific journals very rarely publish studies in which some type of positive change has not been demonstrated. Therefore, the research probably does not include as many instances of either the ineffectiveness or the harmful consequences of receiving sex therapy as occur in actual clinical practice.

Keeping these limitations in mind, the following sections summarize the findings of the research.[5,6] We begin by reporting the range of client improvement in sexual performance from between the time the client or couple entered therapy to when therapy ended. We also report the range of the number of treatment sessions after which clients improved.

Premature Ejaculation

Between 50 and 100% of these men improved their sexual functioning after 10 to 20 sessions. For some men, this meant gaining a sense of voluntary control over when they ejaculated. For others, it meant lasting longer during intercourse even though they may not have been able to control their ejaculation. Some therapists considered treatment successful only if the man could control his ejaculatory response, whereas others measured treatment success by a statistically significant increase in the amount of time from vaginal penetration to ejaculation.

Erection Problems

Anywhere from none to 75% of these men improved, usually after 10 to 20 sessions. Positive outcomes were more likely for men who had been able to gain erections sufficient for intercourse in the past than for those who had never had successful intercourse. Some men improved to the extent that they could penetrate the vagina but not necessarily continue on to ejaculation. Others improved in their ability to gain erections, penetrate, and ejaculate.

In most studies, it was difficult to determine whether these men received comprehensive physical examinations before treatment. It is likely that the physical factors that maintained the erection problems of some of these men were not detected since less sophisticated methods were in use in former years. Whether alcohol or drugs contributed to the erection problems also could not be determined.

Ejaculatory Inhibition

Most of the studies that treated men with ejaculatory inhibition were reports of one or two clients, with treatment lasting between 5 and 20 sessions. In most of these reports, the men were able to ejaculate during intercourse after treatment. Several studies that conducted treatment with a greater number of clients found that between 40 and 50% of the men improved their ability to ejaculate during intercourse. Some men could ejaculate a greater percentage of the time that they had sexual intercourse, while others still could not ejaculate without extended nonintercourse stimulation.

Orgasm Problems

Between 70 and 100% of women who had never reached orgasm could do so through masturbation, usually after 8 to 15 sessions. Most women who reached orgasm from masturbation also learned to do so from a partner's sexual stimulation; however, a smaller proportion of these women reached orgasm from intercourse alone.

Less impressive gains were found for women who had reached orgasm in the past but who no longer did at an acceptable rate with a partner, and for women who reached orgasm from masturbation and/or manual stimulation by a partner but not during intercourse. Anywhere from none to 75% of these women improved their orgasmic frequency after about 10 to 20 sessions.

When a woman did increase her orgasmic frequency during intercourse, it was difficult to determine whether this was due to concurrent manual stimulation of her clitoris, to her partner's ability to last longer in intercourse, or to the woman being more relaxed and responsive during sex. The findings suggested that it may be unrealistic for some women to expect to reach orgasm at a high frequency (e.g., 90% of her attempts) during intercourse without concurrent manual stimulation.

Painful Intercourse or Vaginismus

So little has been reported on women with painful intercourse that we cannot make a definitive statement about outcome. For women with vaginismus, between 66.6 and 100% were able to engage in intercourse, usually after an average of 7 to 14 sessions. It appears, however, that only a small percentage of these women were able to reach orgasm during intercourse.

Sexual Desire and Arousal

We did not find much information on the outcome of clients with sexual desire and arousal problems. Clients who began treatment with a low frequency of masturbation, especially women, increased their rate of masturbation and the frequency of sexual activity with a partner. Persons with low sexual desire reported initiating sex more often, relative to their partner's initiations. They also responded more positively to their partner's sexual advances.[7]

Other Populations

Not much research has explored the effects of sex therapy on the elderly, or on homosexual clients. In one study, elderly couples, almost all of which complained of a specific sex problem (most frequently premature ejaculation or erectile failure), increased their sexual satisfaction and the frequency of engaging in various sexual activities.[8] Another study found that for gay male couples, premature ejaculation had the highest degree of success from sex therapy, followed by erection problems and ejaculatory inhibition.[9] We did not find any studies that evaluated treatment effectiveness on persons with physical disabilities or medical conditions. Therefore, we have only a minimal amount of information on persons who do not represent the mainstream of those typically treated by sex therapists.

Changes in Personal and Relationship Functioning

In general, the studies found that sex therapy decreased sexual anxiety and fostered positive changes in marital adjustment and communication skills. Some clients reported increased sexul satisfaction even if they still had problems with sexual functioning. For example, many women with orgasm problems reported positive changes in their sexual relationship even though they did not increase their ability to reach orgasm during intercourse.

What About Long-Term Changes?

We don't know much about the long-term effects of sex therapy. Most of the follow-ups in the studies that included them were conducted no longer than six months after treatment.

What were the results of the follow-ups? About one-quarter of the studies found that some clients lost their treatment gains over time. In several studies, only about half of the clients maintained their improvement.

The most noteworthy long-term follow-up was conducted by Daniel Goldberg and Marilyn DeAmicis.[10] In 1981, they reported preliminary results of a three-year follow-up of 38 couples, or 42% of the 90 couples who were treated at the Sex Therapy Center at the State University of New York at Stony Brook. The couples, who had various sex problems, were treated for one session per week for 15 weeks.

The researchers found that the clients' reports of their sexual performance and sexual satisfaction fluctuated considerably over the three-year period. Males and females made changes after therapy but showed a gradual relapse to their pretreatment level of functioning on some variables. The women maintained improvement in their ability to reach orgasm through masturbation and from partner stimulation. However, women were not as successful in reaching orgasm through intercourse. Men with erection problems maintained their performance gains even though they still had erection problems in 25% of their sexual interactions. Men with premature ejaculation reported an initial increase in ejaculatory latency that was not maintained; in fact, these men returned to their pretreatment level of performance. With regard to sexual desire, measured by intercourse frequency and desired intercourse frequency, both men and women returned to their pretreatment levels after having improved. The decline in the desired intercourse frequency seemed to be more rapid for men. Over the three-year period, the clients, in general, maintained levels of sexual satisfaction. However, positive changes in sexual performance, in many cases, showed a gradual decline over the three-year period.

Why did the sexual performance of many clients relapse or return to pretreatment levels? The couples may have no longer considered sexual performance to be as much of a priority as it was during and directly after treatment. On the other hand, 15 sessions of treatment may not be sufficiently potent to facilitate lasting improvement in sexual performance. Perhaps sex therapy can do only so much within its typically brief time frame.

Group versus Individual Treatment

Should sex therapy clients be treated in individual sessions or in a group with other clients? Our review of the studies found that the group format seems to be at least as effective as treating an individual or couple separately.[11] Clients participating in group treatment reported that the support and acceptance from other group members as well as others' self-disclosure contributed to their improvement.[12,13] Yet for some clients, especially those who are shy and have difficulty discussing their problems with others, the group may be contraindicated. Individual treatment also may be more effective for clients who need a more concentrated focus on their specific sex problem than is provided in group treatment.

Two Therapists versus One

The sex treatment presented by Masters and Johnson emphasized the value of a male and female therapist team for treating couples. However, no evidence exists that better results are obtained from two therapists, whether male/female or same-sex, than from one therapist of either sex.[14,15] Certainly, a drawback of the male/female therapist team is that it typically is more costly than treatment conducted by one therapist alone. It is our clinical impression that many clients, especially those who do not have a partner, do not necessarily gain more benefits from two therapists versus one. However, for some couples, especially those in which both partners feel more comfortable in being treated by a therapist of the same sex, a male/female therapist team may be more of a factor in facilitating treatment gains. Research is needed to test this assumption.

Daily versus Weekly Treatment

Most clients probably are treated weekly or twice a week for either a predetermined number of sessions or until the client terminates treatment. The choice of time format likely depends upon factors such as each therapist's preferences, the client's finances, and scheduling considerations. Which time format is better? One study addressed this question. No differences were found when the effects of 15 hours of daily versus weekly treatment on various sex problems were contrasted. Some slight evidence was found for the superiority of weekly over daily treatment for women who had previously reached orgasm and men with erection problems.[16] However, more research is needed before a specific time format for a given sex problem can be recommended.

Overall, the research suggests that sex therapy is not equally effective for all clients. Sex therapy has the greatest likelihood of facilitating sexual performance changes and increased sexual satisfaction for men with premature ejaculation and women who had never reached orgasm prior to treatment. There is less likelihood of positive changes occurring for men with erection problems and women who would like to reach orgasm more frequently during intercourse. But the ability of sex therapy to foster long-term changes is still an uncertainty. Of the clients who were followed up, some maintained improvement for months or years while others did not. But we really do not know what happened to the many other clients who were not followed up.

Although sex therapy can have very beneficial effects, we have tried to show in this chapter that the therapy experience is, to some extent, a gamble. A client with high expectations for improvement risks disappointment from sex therapy unless he or she is willing to devote a considerable amount of time and energy to carrying out the homework assignments, and unless a willing, cooperative, and supportive partner is available to help with the exercises. Even then, there are no guarantees. Sex therapy can take a client only so far. Similar to the clients of the other psychotherapies, clients who reflect a fairly positive personal and social adjustment to life before treatment have a much greater likelihood of improving from sex therapy than clients whose sex problems seem to be symptoms of other, long-lasting adjustment difficulties.

REFERENCES

1. S. McMullen, R. D. Rosen, "Self-Administered Masturbation Training in the Treatment of Primary Orgasmic Dysfunction," *Journal of Consulting and Clinical Psychology* 47 (1979), pp. 912–918.
2. T. H. Van Wyke, "Relationship of Time Spent on Masturbation Assignments with Orgasmic Outcome in Preorgasmic Women's Groups," *Journal of Sex Research* 18 (1982), pp. 33–40.
3. B. Zilbergeld, *The Shrinking of America* (Boston: Little, Brown, 1983).
4. N. Payn, J. Wakefield, "The Effect of Group Treatment of Primary Orgasmic Dysfunction on the Marital Relationship," *Journal of Sex and Marital Therapy* 8 (1982), pp. 135–150.
5. Perhaps the most difficult problem in evaluating the findings was that the studies differed in the criteria used to define a treatment success. Depending upon the study, "improvement" sometimes referred to whether the client met the therapist's standard of improved performance, whether the client reported improvement,

or whether clients' treatment goals were met. Some studies presented their results in "success rates." This does not provide the specific information that we need in order to know precisely what happened. An example should underscore this point. Let us suppose that there are eight women receiving instruction in masturbation training methods. By the end of treatment, all but one of the women regularly could reach orgasm through masturbation. Some researchers would define this as an 87.5% "success rate." Three or four of the women might have shown their partners how they like to be stimulated and also could reach orgasm when their partners stimulated them manually or orally. Two of these women also might be able to reach orgasm during intercourse. If the criterion of "treatment success" was reaching orgasm regularly through intercourse, then the "success rate" for this group would be considered only 25%. It is clear that although seven of the eight women made positive treatment gains, their levels of "success" were very different.

6. More than one-third of the studies assessed the impact of treatment on a single client or couple. In these studies, not much can be said with confidence about whether the findings are relevant to similar individuals or couples. More than three-fourths of the studies, including the single case study reports, evaluated less than 25 clients. In the studies that treated more than a few clients, treatment outcome often was evaluated by statistically significant improvement on questionnaires or rating scales from pre- to posttherapy. In these studies, only the average change for all of the clients in the study was reported; this made it impossible to determine the outcome for each client who received treatment. Of course, statistically significant improvement on a questionnaire for a group of clients does not necessarily mean that each client improved. Instead, it is more likely that some of the clients improved a great deal, some improved slightly, others did not change at all, and still others actually deteriorated in functioning. These differential outcomes are not specific to sex therapy clients but also are typical of therapy clients in general.

7. L. R. Schover, J. LoPiccolo, "Treatment Effectiveness for Dysfunctions of Sexual Desire," *Journal of Sex and Marital Therapy* 8 (1982), pp. 179–197.

8. K. F. Rowland, S. N. Haynes, "A Sexual Enhancement Program for Elderly Couples," *Journal of Sex and Marital Therapy* 4 (1978), pp. 91–113.

9. D. P. McWhirter, M. Mattison, "The Treatment of Sexual Dysfunc-

tions in Gay Male Couples," *Journal of Sex and Marital Therapy* 4 (1978), pp. 213–218.

10. D. C. Goldberg, M. A. DeAmicis, "Factors Influencing the Lasting Effectiveness of Sex Therapy" (Paper presented at the American Psychological Association's 89th Annual Convention, Los Angeles, August 1981).

11. K. H. Mills, P. R. Kilmann, "Group Treatment of Sexual Dysfunctions: A Methodological Review of the Outcome Literature," *Journal of Sex and Marital Therapy* 8 (1982), pp. 259–296.

12. G. H. Nemetz, K. D. Craig, G. Reith, "Treatment of Female Sexual Dysfunction Through Symbolic Modeling," *Journal of Consulting and Clinical Psychology* 46 (1978), pp. 62–73.

13. B. S. Reynolds, B. D. Cohen, D. B. Schochet, S. C. Price, A. J. Anderson, "Dating Skills Training in the Group Treatment of Erectile Dysfunction for Men Without Partners," *Journal of Sex and Marital Therapy* 7 (1981), pp. 184–194.

14. M. J. Crowe, P. Gillan, S. Golombok, "Form and Content in the Conjoint Treatment of Sexual Dysfunction: A Controlled Study," *Behaviour Research and Therapy* 19 (1981), pp. 47–54.

15. J. LoPiccolo, "Effects of Variations in Format on Sex Therapy Outcome" (Paper presented at the Society for Sex Therapy and Research meeting, Charleston, S.C., June 1982).

16. J. R. Heiman, J. LoPiccolo, "Clinical Outcomes of Sex Therapy: Effects of Daily Versus Weekly Treatment" (Unpublished manuscript,1982).

Chapter Eight

THE GROWTH OF SEX THERAPY: BENEFITS AND PITFALLS

Sex therapy has taken on many new dimensions and characteristics since it was introduced by Masters and Johnson in 1970. Sex therapists now treat a greater variety of sexual problems, many of which are much more complex to treat than initially was assumed.

Sex therapy, in part, has grown out of necessity. The influence of the sexual liberation movement has helped to create new ways of viewing sexual behavior, with new expectations and demands. Many men and women now expect sex to be a part of dating, and for some individuals, an essential part. The media tend to emphasize the ultimate sexual potential of both men and women. For many, this has created excessive anxiety about sexual performance. More men and women are expecting sexual satisfaction from a relationship. They feel freer to ask for it, and they feel freer to voice their disappointment, and even resentment, when they do not get it. Many couples are examining their sexual relationship in a way that couples 20 years ago did not. This has created a ready and willing market for sex therapy.

The way that sex therapy has grown is similar to the pattern of growth of any new psychotherapy. Initially, sex therapy was hailed as "the answer." Gradually, more and more professionals joined the bandwagon and began to use the methods. Researchers began to investigate whether sex therapy actually was as effective as its advocates claimed.

A sizable number of studies were published, after which their findings were evaluated. The conclusion, which applies to the other psychotherapies as well, is that sex therapy can be effective, but much less often than initially was thought. It is not really clear which treatment methods are superior, even for clients who have a greater probability of success, such as women who have never reached orgasm or men who can't control their ejaculation.

It also is important to emphasize that sex therapy likely is ineffective in producing long-term change for many people, regardless of the problem. Often, its successes are only temporary, not the absolute cures that people initially assumed would occur. A considerable degree of backsliding or relapse for many clients is possible, if not probable. Some clients even are harmed in some way after having received sex therapy.[1]

Regardless of this risk, however, sex therapy seems to be the most cost-effective method for treating sex problems. It typically is conducted in a relatively short period of time in comparison with some of the other psychotherapies. Hence, even when sex therapy fails, at least clients have not spent their entire life, or life savings, to find out that their goals for improvement are unrealistic or that they cannot be helped.

Sex therapists are very visible today. Many offer information and advice about sexual matters in articles and books, and in interviews with various media sources. Some sex therapists regularly appear on television and radio talk shows. Even though some people may have misinterpreted the advice offered by sex therapists through the media, in general it certainly can be said that sex therapists provide a noteworthy service by informing the public about sexuality. Undoubtedly, many more people know more about sexual anatomy and physiology, and about sexual functioning in general, as a direct result of the growth of sex

therapy. Mental health professionals have a greater reali-
zation of the negative impact of a sex problem on a person's self-esteem, and that for many couples, sexual satisfaction is an important contribution to overall relationship
satisfaction.

The growth of sex therapy, however, has not occurred
without certain pitfalls. Sex therapists have added to the
very performance anxiety that they often treat by implying
that it is not possible to have a fulfilling sex life without
reaching orgasms or ejaculations, and/or engaging in more
frequent sex and in many new ways. For some clients,
attempting to follow this sexual performance model
undoubtedly has created difficulties in areas where there
were none. An example might be a couple who is quite
content with having sex once per week in a similar way
each time. Such a couple would experience considerable
pressure from a therapist who believes that their sexual
relationship could be enhanced by having sex three times
a week and by adding a variety of sexual activities to their
repertoire. Sex therapists often encourage their clients to
masturbate, even though some feel very uncomfortable
doing so. Some sex therapists encourage some clients to
have sex with more than one partner; this has been harmful for clients who are not comfortable in having sex in the
first place. Many sex therapists stress the importance of
strengthening pelvic musculature to aid women in reaching orgasm. Women who did not have more orgasms, or
did not reach orgasm more quickly after strengthening
their pelvic muscles, may have become more anxious or
felt more inadequate after treatment.[1]

The strong impact of the beliefs and discoveries of
prominent professionals on standards of sexual performance has been shown over the years. Around the turn of
the 20th century, psychoanalyst Sigmund Freud proposed
the existence of two separate female orgasmic responses,

clitoral and vaginal. As a consequence, many women at that time felt anxious and inadequate if they did not have vaginal orgasms. Many of these women, even though they might have been able to have clitoral orgasms, were encouraged to enter long-term psychoanalysis so that they could resolve the conflicts that presumably were inhibiting their vaginal sensitivity. In 1966, Masters and Johnson's *Human Sexual Response*[2] suggested that all female orgasms required clitoral stimulation, either from direct or indirect means, and that there was no physiological basis for more than one basic type of female orgasm. This type of orgasm is known as a *vulval orgasm*. With all the publicity given to clitoral orgasms, many sex therapists emphasized the importance of clitoral orgasms and encouraged women to have them. As a consequence, many women who were not reaching orgasm from clitoral stimulation began to feel anxious and inadequate.

A new source of sexual "performance anxiety" may be just around the corner. In the early 1980s, clinical observations reported by various writers, including John Perry and Beverly Whipple,[3] added new information to the yet-to-be-resolved controversy involving one type versus two types of female orgasm. These writers suggested that there may be a second type of female orgasm, referred to as a *uterine orgasm*. This type of orgasm presumably could be reached from the stimulation of a small, sensitive, possibly glandular structure located within the anterior wall of the vagina close to the cervix, which is sensitive to intravaginal stimulation. Perry and Whipple named this area the "Grafenberg spot" after the physician who first described it in 1950. The writers reported on one woman who reached orgasms from the stimulation of this area without any concurrent clitoral stimulation. These orgasms, which were felt deep inside her pelvis, were characterized by the expulsion or ejaculation of a "prostatic" fluid through the urethra. This was not presumed to be an indication of urinary stress incontinence, nor a sign of urinary tract or genital disorders.

Subsequent research by Daniel Goldberg and his associates[4] cast doubt on the existence of the area in all women. Some areas apparently occur in a transverse fashion, while others seemingly occur from front to back. In some women, the area was found to be located in the front or in the back of the vaginal wall. The researchers could not always locate the area, suggesting that it is an anatomical variation found in some women but not in others.

Goldberg's research also suggested that the area and the emission of fluid upon orgasm may have been inadvertently connected. Some women may have an area in their vagina that serves as a source of pleasure when stimulated during intercourse, but they may not ejaculate. Others may experience "ejaculation," but the area cannot be located in their vagina. In Goldberg's sample of women, the ejaculate and urine seemed to be the same. It is possible that women who emit fluid through the urethra upon reaching orgasm may actually have urinary stress incontinence.

Much is not known of the actual physiological and psychological mechanisms associated with "female ejaculation." Yet there has been a considerable amount of premature publicity surrounding this phenomenon. Papers on the topic have been presented in scientific meetings throughout the country. A book entitled *The G-Spot and Other Recent Discoveries About Human Sexuality* was published in 1982.[5] Female ejaculation has been discussed in the news media, in popular magazines, and on television talk shows. All of this publicity has led many women and their partners to search for the presumed area in the vagina, and to discover whether the sensations from its stimulation are more satisfying than other types of sexual stimulation. The "Grafenberg spot" and the exaggerated emphasis given to it already have caused considerable frustration. Some sex therapists have received letters from women who are upset because they have been unable to find this "G-spot." The scant research on female ejaculation suggests that sex therapists should communicate to the public that the stimulation of the "G-spot" merely is a sexual variation for some women and their partners, and that women who are unable to ejaculate do not have a sexual problem. It is evident that the media's exaggerated emphasis on sexual performance can inhibit a person's sense of freedom to discover individualized ways to enjoy sex.

At present, sex therapy is still an art rather than a science. Regardless of the potential pitfalls, it has helped many clients to overcome their sexual problems and to lead a more fulfilling life. As with many new fields of endeavor, sex therapy is still growing and it is fraught with many unresolved issues. We have made great strides in discovering methods to treat sexual problems, but we still have much to learn.

REFERENCES

1. B. Zilbergeld, personal communication (Oakland: June 1982).
2. W. H. Masters, V. E. Johnson, *Human Sexual Response* (Boston: Little, Brown, 1966).
3. J. Perry, B. Whipple, "Pelvic Muscle Strength of Female Ejaculators: Evidence in Support of a New Theory of Orgasm," *Journal of Sex Research* 17(1) (February 1981), pp. 22–39.
4. D. Goldberg, B. Whipple, R. Fishkin, J. Waxman, S. Wolf, M. A. Rubie, P. Fink, "Female Ejaculation: A Review of Initial Hypotheses" (Paper presented at the Society for Sex Therapy and Research, Charleston,

   S.C., June 1982).
5. A. K. Ladas, B. Whipple, J. D. Perry, *The G-Spot and Other Recent Dis-coveries About Human Sexuality* (New York: Holt, Rinehart & Winston, 1982).

INDEX

Erection problems
   definition of, 89
   differences among men with, 89–90
   drugs and, 90
   goals of treatment with, 94
   homework assignments and, 50
   intercourse and, 96
   physical causes of, 90–92
   psychological causes of, 91–92
   relationships and, 96
   research of, 203
   sensate focus and, 96
   surgery and, 99–101
   systematic desensitization and, 57–58
   treatment of, 92–99

Fair-fight training, 54
Frigidity, definition of, 17

G-Spot, 218–220

Homosexuals
   research of treatment with, 205–206
   sex therapy and, 175–176
   sexual problems and, 175

Kidney disease
   sex therapy and, 182
   sexual problems and, 181–182

Orgasm problems
   causes of, 115–119
   partners and, 118–119
   relationships and, 119
   research of, 204

Sex therapist
    certification requirements of, 33–35
    definition of, 33–35
Sex therapy
    cost of, 32
    elderly and, 173–175
    erection problems and, 92–99
    evolution of, 16–25
    daily vs. weekly, 209–210
    factors of, 31–32
    group vs. individual treatment and, 208
    growth of, 215–220
    homework assignments and, 49–53, 56
    individual and relationship functioning and, 206
    individual vs. sexual problems, 59–62
    long-term effects of, 206–208
    long-term treatment and, 22
    methods of, 22, 31–73
    physical disabilities and, 176–184
    relationship vs. sex problems and, 62–64
    session lengths of, 32
    sex education and, 48–49
    sex history and, 35–37
    treatment failure and, 194–202
    treatment success and, 189–194
    vs. other psychotherapies, 69–73
Sexual arousal
    definition of, 156
    desire and, 156
    differences in, 31
    factors influencing, 157
    research of, 21–22, 205
    treatment of, 157–161
Sexual desire
    definition of, 142
    differences with partners and, 143–144